The American Destiny
Volume 14

The Great Depression

The Great Depression

The American Destiny

An Illustrated History of the United States

Editor in Chief
Henry Steele Commager

Editors
Marcus Cunliffe
Maldwyn A. Jones
Edward Horton

Orbis · London

EDITOR IN CHIEF: Henry Steele Commager, now Professor Emeritus at Amherst College, has taught at Columbia, Cambridge, Oxford and other universities. In a long and illustrious career he has written many books in his own right, including *Theodore Parker, The American Mind, Majority Rule and Minority Rights*, and *The Empire of Reason*. He is the co-author (with Samuel Eliot Morison) of *The Growth of the American Republic*, editor of *Documents of American History*, and (with Richard B. Morris) of the fifty-volume *New American Nation* series.

SENIOR EDITORS: Marcus Cunliffe, now University Professor at George Washington University, and formerly of Manchester and Sussex Universities, has also taught at Harvard and Michigan. His books include *The Literature of the United States, George Washington: Man and Monument, Soldier and Civilians, The American Presidency*, and *Chattel Slavery and Wage Slavery*. Maldwyn A. Jones is Commonwealth Fund Professor of American History at the University of London. He has been a visiting professor at Harvard and at the Universities of Chicago and Pennsylvania. He has written extensively on American ethnic groups. His books include *American Immigration*, a volume in the *Chicago History of American Civilization*, and *The Limits of Liberty: American History, 1607-1980*.

Published in the United Kingdom by
Orbis Book Publishing Corporation Ltd.
3rd Floor Greater London House
Hampstead Road
London NW1 7QX
England

ISBN 0 356 12944 6

Contributors to this volume include: David Burner, State University of New York, Stony Brook; Richard S. Kirkendall, Iowa State University; Theodore Saloutos, University of California, Los Angeles; Jordan A. Schwarz, Northern Illinois University; Marcus Cunliffe, George Washington University; Rhodri Jeffreys-Jones, University of Edinburgh; Esmond Wright, former Director, Institute of United States Studies, London.

Printed in Yugoslavia.

Introduction

In the fall of 1929 the American people suffered the worst economic disaster in their history. There had been several earlier depressions but this one was infinitely more severe and it affected a larger segment of the population. It also lasted longer. After the Wall Street crash the economy spiralled remorselessly downward for three grim years. Businesses went bankrupt, banks failed, and one quarter of the work force lost their jobs.

The Great Depression was not unique to the United States. It was an experience shared by every industrialized country with the exception of the Soviet Union. But for Americans the depression was psychologically more shattering than for other peoples because it was in such contrast to what had gone before. Hitherto the whole history of the United States had been one of unparalleled and continuously increasing prosperity. During the 1920s Americans had come to enjoy the highest standard of material well-being ever attained anywhere. Then, almost overnight, the country was plunged into destitution.

By the winter of 1932–33 despair was almost universal. Unemployment reached 15 million, there were bread lines in the cities and angry mobs of farmers in the countryside; vast numbers of people were living in shantytowns or were drifting aimlessly about. City governments found the problem of relief beyond them and nothing the Hoover administration had done—and it was more than any previous administration had attempted—had prevented the depression from getting steadily worse. At this time of misery and discontent some Americans began to wonder whether their political and economic institutions could survive, whether indeed democracy and private enterprise capitalism ought not to be replaced by something else—communism or fascism perhaps. There was even talk of revolution.

But although in parts of Europe the depression fatally weakened the political and social structure, there was to be no revolution in America. Instead there occurred that astonishing outburst of experimentation, improvisation, and reform presided over by Franklin D. Roosevelt and known as the New Deal. In electing Roosevelt to the presidency in 1932 Americans had no reason to expect anything startling or novel. His record did not suggest that he possessed exceptional gifts of leadership and he had not yet defined the New Deal except in the vaguest and most general terms. But the moment he took office he acted—and acted decisively. During the "Hundred Days" there was a tidal wave of executive and legislative activity aimed at relief, recovery, and reform. They marked the beginning of five dramatic and controversial years. By 1938, when growing preoccupation with world affairs brought the New Deal to a close, Congress had enacted a mass of social and economic legislation greater in volume and complexity than that of any other period in the nation's history.

These measures were not based upon any coherent or consistent body of doctrine, but were essentially tentative and pragmatic. Moreover their provisions were often contradictory and overlapping. Hence the character of the New Deal remains difficult to define and historians have been unable to agree whether it represented a revolution or whether it grew naturally out of the American reform tradition. Nor is there unanimity about its effects or about FDR's role.

The verdict of the American people at the time was one of overwhelming approval. Though Roosevelt was denounced by an embittered minority as a dictator and accused of undermining American institutions, the mass of the voters took him to their hearts and he was three times reelected. This despite the fact that the New Deal had obvious limitations and failures. It did not, for example, restore real prosperity. The most Roosevelt could claim was to have alleviated suffering and to have brought about a partial recovery. Nevertheless the New Deal had substituted hope for despair and had restored the faith of Americans in their institutions.

The New Deal conditioned the thinking of an entire generation of Americans. It also brought permanent changes to American life. It greatly enhanced the scope of the federal government's activities. It established the principle that the regulation of the economy was a governmental responsibility. It laid the foundations of a broad welfare program and conferred a new status on labor. And it produced a major realignment in American political parties. By putting together a coalition of the disadvantaged, Roosevelt ensured that the Democrats took the place of the Republicans as the normal majority party.

Contents

Chapter I

A NATION IN DESPAIR

Prosperity was the keynote when Herbert Hoover entered the White House in 1929. The optimism of the twenties promised more and better for everyone, but within a year the nation had plunged into the greatest depression in its history. To Hoover, the slump differed little from those that had occurred before. Recovery, he said, was "just around the corner." But events proved otherwise. The Wall Street crash led to more bankruptcies, more unemployment, more insecurity. By the election of 1932, the number of unemployed totaled well over 10 million. The people had had enough: they wanted a new man willing to try new ideas. And they got one.

The Onset of Depression

In one respect at least the 1928 campaign followed a normal pattern. The presidential candidate of the party in power campaigned on the assumption that most Americans enjoyed prosperity and would reap greater prosperity if they elected him. "Today there are almost nine automobiles for each ten families, where seven and one-half years ago only enough automobiles were running to average less than four for each ten families," Herbert Hoover declared. "The slogan of progress is changing from the full dinner pail to the full garage. Our people have more to eat, better things to wear, and better homes. . . . All this progress means far more than increased creature comforts. It binds a thousand interpretations into a greater and fuller life." The times were so good that Hoover could boast that "we have been forced to find a new definition for poverty." He suggested that the trend had to continue upward because "never in our history was the leadership in our economic life more distinguished in its abilities than today, and it has grown greatly in its consciousness of public responsibility."

These stilted expressions of confidence ignored real signs of trouble. Over 5,000 banks failed in the twenties, 669 of them in 1927. Although farm prices had risen slowly over the previous few years, thousands of farmers had gone broke and the purchasing power of the farmers who survived the agricultural depression was still below what it had been in 1913. No reliable labor statistics are available, but unemployment was estimated at close to 2 million, roughly 7 per cent of the working force. Hourly wages were 8 per cent higher than in 1923, but profits had risen by 62 per cent, only one of many indications that prosperity was not broadly distributed. Home construction had been declining since 1927. Yet some producers acted as if consumers abounded. In 1929 Detroit manufactured more automobiles than ever before.

Wall Street behaved as if the best was still to come. Between 1927, when the Federal Reserve loosened credit, and September 1929, prices of industrial stocks had doubled. In 1929 alone, Radio Corporation of America stock soared from $94.50 a share to $505. RCA was exceptional, although speculation in automobile, steel, rubber, glass, and electrical manufactures was not lagging too far behind. But in September, the stock market broke, then steadied before prices fell sharply again in late October. On October 29, the panic to sell was on. Some prices fell by as much as thirty or forty dollars. By the end of the year the industrial price average had fallen by about a quarter in only three months.

The Wall Street crash was a principal factor in causing the Great Depression. Part of the decline can be traced to the stock market's psychological influence, but a great deal of it was due to lost investments. Mortgage money

and manufacturing output suffered sharp losses. Although the slide leveled out in early 1930, it turned sharply downward soon after. Moreover, it was a worldwide depression. President Hoover later blamed the depression's origins on foreign economic conditions. There is some truth to that, especially if the roots of collapse are traced back to the First World War's devastation and subsequent debts and reparations. Germany, a major industrial nation, had gone through terrible hardships in the 1920s and its unemployment rate was considerably higher than America's. But inherent weaknesses in the United States economy meant that once the depression

began it would be worse here than anywhere else.

Hoover acted quickly to stop the depression. Inviting prominent industrialists to confer with him at the White House, Hoover won pledges from them not to slash wages or lay off workers. He urged them to maintain their confidence in the essential strength of the economy and cooperate with him by not reducing production. Confidence and cooperation always remained his watchwords. Without them he believed further decline was possible and recovery unlikely. For the time being businessmen sustained Hoover's faith in the system. By June 1930 he was certain that recovery had begun.

He was wrong. Unemployment grew rapidly the rest of that year, passing 5 million in September, 8 million in January 1931, 9 million in October. In 1931 the Ford Motor Company cut its payroll from 84,000 workers to 37,000. The textile industry collapsed in New England and the city of New Bedford, Massachusetts, was bankrupt. By 1932, there were a million unemployed in New

The Great Depression ruined careers and sapped the vitality of people everywhere. Life for those without jobs or homes, as portrayed in Reginald Marsh's The Park Bench, *suddenly turned sour.*

Private or municipal "breadlines" (left) proliferated during the depression, when no federal program of social security or relief existed. At the same time, families lacking the financial resources to keep up rent or mortgage payments shifted into shantytowns or "Hoovervilles" (right). Constructed from bits of corrugated iron, planks, and whatever building material could be found, crude dwellings such as these gave shelter to thousands of desperate Americans.

York City where homeless men and women slept in subway stations, telephone booths and in parks. At Seventy-fourth Street and Riverside Drive, a squatters' colony dubbed "Hoover Village" erected homes made of used boards, sheets of corrugated tin, strips of tar paper and wire alongside the Hudson River and within view of a steel magnate's mansion. Other "Hoovervilles" were built by the jobless and the homeless in New York City's Central Park, Chicago's Grant Park, and elsewhere. In Cleveland 50 per cent were out of work, 80 per cent in Toledo, 660,000 in Chicago, and in Donora, Pennsylvania, only 277 of 13,900 workers held regular jobs.

For most of the unemployed there was little relief. In 1930 the International Apple Shippers Association hit upon the idea of marketing their surplus apples on the street corners of cities by consigning a crate of apples to the unemployed who sold apples for five cents apiece with the slogan, "Buy an apple a day and eat the depression away!" Some 6,000 people sold apples on New York City streets in 1930. By the end of the year a rise in apple prices made it unprofitable for the jobless. Charitable organizations like the Salvation Army and the YMCA set up soup kitchens as well as breadlines; long lines of unemployed people seeking some nourishment appeared in cities across the nation.

They got no relief from Washington. The Hoover administration's relief policy dictated that private, local,

and state institutions had to be the first sources of relief. That made sense early in the depression but it became evident by 1931 that philanthropy was drying up and local relief sources were exhausted. New York, Chicago, Philadelphia, and Detroit were too much in debt to sustain their relief rolls. Chicago had to fire police and firemen while its teachers continued without salary.

President Hoover was not indifferent to the crisis. He created the President's Emergency Committee for Employment whose task it was to encourage state and local governments to accelerate their public works plans. Private institutions were likewise urged to undertake work projects. Aside from documenting the need for relief and aiding the Red Cross in 1930–31, PECE did little more than encourage other agencies to accomplish what their meager means prevented them from doing. Federal funds were needed but Hoover refused to ask Congress for relief appropriations or approve any congressional relief initiatives. He feared the expenditures would create budget deficits so large as to disrupt business confidence or set in motion an uncontrollable inflation. Also, he had done no more in the 1921 depression, when he was Harding's secretary of commerce, and that had been enough for recovery. He honestly expected an upturn would soon be apparent as it was nearly a decade before.

Recovery, however, was not around the corner. More and more people blamed Hoover for their plight. The president

became the butt of bitter humor. Aside from the Hoover-ville shantytowns, people called empty pockets turned inside out "Hoover flags." A comedian told a story of the time Hoover was away from the White House and asked his secretary for a nickel to call a friend from a telephone booth. "Here's a dime," responded the secretary. "Call all your friends." A young man hitchhiked from California to New York in only five days by carrying a sign reading, "Give me a ride or I'll vote for Hoover." In one vaudeville routine the straight man said: "Business is improving." The comedian asked: "Is Hoover dead?" It is

A run on the banks followed the Wall Street crash. Below: Depositors line up in the hope of withdrawing their funds. Right: An official assures a crowd of his bank's soundness.

said that Babe Ruth refused to have his salary cut $10,000 from $80,000; a friend told him that he had a bigger salary than the president, to which Ruth snapped: "So what? I had a better season than he did." A ditty of the times went:

> Mellon pulled the whistle,
> Hoover rang the bell.
> Wall Street gave the signal
> And the country went to hell.

Help for the Economy

A turning point in the early depression came during the spring of 1931 when the Creditanstalt in Vienna, Austria's largest bank, collapsed after the French removed their vital short-term credit support. Germany was hit hard, and in June Hoover announced a moratorium of one year on payments of all foreign debts. The moratorium, it was hoped, would boost foreign trade which had been weakened by the Smoot-Hawley tariff of 1930. For a brief while Americans found the moratorium action a psychological stimulant. But in September, Great Britain went off the gold standard. That set Europeans to exchanging their dollars for United States gold. American credit reserves were threatened and the already weakened banking system was thrown into greater jeopardy. Bank runs and failures increased spectacularly; 522 commercial banks with $471 million in deposits suspended dealings during October 1931. Some banks had to close in order to prevent massive withdrawals. A

novice *New York Times* reporter proudly deposited his first pay check and upon leaving the bank he spied a sign reading "Deposits Only, No Withdrawals;" he raced back to the teller, too late to retrieve his money.

Hoover had to act to save the banks. The president wanted to organize relief for the banks along the same lines he organized relief for the unemployed—relying upon the voluntary cooperation of the community. For the bankers this meant that the strong banks should pool their resources and save the weak banks. Pittsburgh bankers, for instance, had raised three or four million dollars in an effort to save a prominent bank in the steel city. Hoover asked Andrew Mellon, a Pittsburgh banker, to contribute a million dollars to the emergency fund; Mellon refused. Could Hoover expect other bankers to contribute to a bank relief fund if Mellon, his own secretary of the Treasury, failed him?

In October, Hoover tested voluntary cooperation in a capitalist society with the big capitalists themselves. He met with representatives of J. P. Morgan and Company and other New York investment bankers. Hoover asked the bankers to create the National Credit Corporation, a credit pool of $500 million contributed by banks for the purpose of giving loans to weakened banks. The bankers were agreeable, but only if Hoover met their terms: they wanted the restoration of the War Finance Corporation, the 1918 federal credit agency that had subsidized exports until 1929. This was a defeat for Hoover's voluntary cooperation. The bankers wanted loans from the federal Treasury to help save banking, a task Hoover had designated for private sources. But Hoover struck a bargain; he agreed to ask Congress for the new WFC if the bankers organized their NCC. Both agencies were to be capitalized at $500 million.

In January 1932, Congress created the Reconstruction Finance Corporation "to provide emergency financing facilities for financial institutions to aid in financing agriculture, commerce and industry." Many congressmen were angry that Hoover would consider relief for the banks but not for the unemployed. To them it was indicative of Hoover's "trickle-down" theory of the economy: if big business prospered, then eventually there would be work for others. The government would first save the bankers, who would save industry until the system created enough jobs for workers. For Hoover, as economically knowledgeable a president as the nation ever elected, this was the only way to save the system without seriously altering it. Still, his perspective assumed that bankers had enough social responsibility not to use the two loan agencies simply to cut their own losses. The government loans were designed to keep the weak credit institutions in business and thereby make them and the industrial system productive again.

In 1932 the NCC hardly functioned at all and most of the RFC's money went to the big banks. In June, Charles Dawes, president of the RFC and a Chicago banker, resigned from the agency and returned to Chicago. Three weeks later his bank applied for a loan. The RFC granted one of $90 million on condition Chicago bankers contribute an additional $5 million. Because Congress required the RFC to make its loans public, there was an outcry over what appeared to be special treatment given to the former RFC head's bank, even if the bank was vital to the second city's economy. What did not become public knowledge was the abortive effort made by Dawes to use the money to pay off his debtors without assurances that the bank would continue in business as a result of the RFC loan.

Bankers increasingly became the object of enormous public scorn. The city of New York could not maintain its relief rolls and asked Wall Street bankers for a loan to finance its social obligations; the bankers agreed—if the city would slash its relief rolls! "The average citizen always suspected the morals of the financial hierarchy," a reporter wrote, "but now his distrust goes deeper; he doubts its intelligence." One popular yarn described how a banker begged a friend not to reveal his profession to his mother: "She thinks I'm playing the piano in a sporting house." As for Hoover's scheme for the voluntary cooperation of banks, even the president had to admit that it was "difficult to secure cooperation from the financial institutions of the country who have little cohesion and little leadership." The RFC had been hailed as a turning point in public confidence but it remained to be shown that it would restore prosperity.

Meanwhile the depression deepened in the spring of 1932. That year immigration declined and more than three times as many persons left the United States as entered it. America no longer seemed the land of opportunity. People were evicted from their farms and homes because they could not meet the mortgage or tax payments. In one extreme case a Chicago municipal employee lost his home because he could not pay $34 in taxes at a time when the city owed him $850 in unpaid salary. Houses and buildings deteriorated for lack of maintenance. Whether suicides actually increased or not, talk of suicides increased a great deal.

But it should also be pointed out that not everybody suffered. For millions of people, earning a livelihood was more difficult, but life was not desperate. Small businessmen and professionals had less business and found bill collecting more difficult. Many rich people partied as if nothing had happened. And for those fortunate enough to have retained their jobs or to have quickly found new employment, nothing had happened. For some there was

This Chicago woman was typical of thousands who found themselves evicted from home, lodgings, or farm. The trauma of the early 1930s placed many families and individuals under great stress.

My compliments on your
very good taste, sir

Why Miss Anne Gould, daughter of
Mr. and Mrs. Jay Gould, prefers Camels

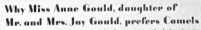
Camel's costlier tobaccos are Milder

for the good things
smoking can give you
Chesterfield
Wins

Drink
Coca-Cola
Delicious and
Refreshing

So refreshing
and so easily served

Guests feel more at home when you manage hospitality easily. That's where ice-cold Coca-Cola comes in. Coca-Cola is so easy to serve…and everybody welcomes its life and sparkle—its pure, wholesome refreshment.

p. s. A drink so good by itself is a natural partner of good things to eat.

FROSTY BOTTLES FROM
YOUR OWN REFRIGERATOR

Despite the severity of the
slump, business continued
to be profitable in some
unexpected areas of the
economy. The advertising
industry, for example, far
from being destroyed,
fared surprisingly well.
Advertisements such as
these appeared in magazines
and on billboards during
the thirties.

always opportunity. Two young men named William Benton and Chester Bowles started an advertising firm early in the depression that made them both rich enough by the end of the 1930s to enable them to devote their lives to public service. Although cold smokestacks dotted the industrial landscape, the tobacco industry thrived thanks to increased cigarette smoking.

Nevertheless, business as usual is not what characterized the times. It was the worst depression in history and the quest for prosperity went on. Panaceas abounded. Some advocated technocracy, turning over the economic system to engineers who would run everything with maximum efficiency—even at the price of freedom. Others were convinced that capitalism had to be replaced with socialism or communism; after all, the Soviets claimed to have no unemployment. Others wanted a strong dose of economic planning that amounted to cartelization. Some suggested that Americans had to create a new form of government, one more efficient, authoritarian, and based on economic representation. Simple solutions were plentiful. More jobs could be created by deporting all aliens. A whimsical economist suggested that a group of millionaires could employ thousands to bail out Long Island Sound. One man told a senator that the government could put men to work moving the Rocky Mountains. Always there were people preaching the gospel of "Buy Now!"— even though others asked "With What?"

To a multitude of Americans it seemed that the Hoover administration should have been doing more in 1932. The president insisted that he was doing all that a free society should expect of its leadership. He was organizing the voluntary forces of the community and encouraging state and local leadership. Those individuals who expected more from Washington were courting socialism or statism —state economic control. Federal action, he warned, would deprive individuals of their initiative and turn them into wards of the government. To the advocates of federal public works, he retorted that they were too late with their plans. In the twenties he had been a prime advocate of public works planning. But once the crisis had begun, he insisted that it was too late to begin projects. Planning required a reservoir of funds and blueprints in the files. Projects begun in 1932 would have no economic impact for eighteen months. The federal Treasury would be exhausted by the projects and, if prosperity returned, they would be inflationary. The government, Hoover declared, could no more legislate against the depression than it could against a Caribbean hurricane. Nature had to take its course without outside interference.

In a move calculated to prevent Congress from legislating its intervention with economic forces, Hoover made a balanced federal budget his primary political issue of 1932. For two years the federal government had suffered declining revenues and budget deficits. Now, in a worse year, Hoover demanded that Congress restrain federal spending and find additional income. Business would be reassured and its confidence restored; it would again invest its capital. Hoover was not alone in his belief that such strategy had double wisdom, politically and economically. The bipartisan leadership of Congress agreed with him. Somehow the budget would be balanced with the introduction of a national manufacturers' sales tax.

But the sales tax frightened the majority of lawmakers. It was a regressive "spending" tax that would add to the cost of ordinary items which depression-plagued citizens already could barely afford. A few politicians questioned the wisdom of a balanced budget and recalled that spending far exceeded revenues during the First World War emergency; was not the depression a crisis similar to the war? Most congressmen, however, agreed with the goal of a balanced budget—if only it could be accomplished without the innovation of the sales tax. Not only did the tax weigh disproportionately upon the shoulders of the poor, it threatened to rob impoverished state governments of a lucrative fiscal device. Several southern states were experimenting with it in an effort to collect enough revenues to pay off their debts and sustain services. Midwestern states, in debt from heavy road-building begun in the twenties, were watching their southern agrarian brethren with a view towards imitating them. Politically, the income tax had become the preserve of the federal government; the sales tax could not be taken from the states or it would bankrupt them.

On April 1, the House of Representatives turned against the White House and congressional leadership and rejected the sales tax in favor of higher corporate, excise, and income taxes. The Revenue Act of 1932 was the most progressive tax law of the decade. Nevertheless, Congress had reaffirmed the validity of a balanced budget.

Sentiment on public works spending then began a decisive shift. A new consensus for using the RFC as a source of public works loans arose in Congress. Retreating in face of the growing popularity of public works, Hoover distinguished between productive projects and nonproductive "pork barrel" political projects for the lawmakers' districts. A productive project not only employed workers in its construction; it created more work by being useful to industry and commerce. A hydroelectric dam or a highway would be reproductive for business; a post office or courthouse would not.

While congressmen could understand his economic distinctions, they favored the political wisdom of work relief projects. The jobless had to be given new jobs right away. Otherwise a generation of unemployed Americans would be sacrificed on the alter of compassionless economic principles. In June, Hoover vetoed a "pork barrel" public works bill and weeks later approved a measure that met his specifications. The Emergency Relief and Construction Act of 1932 guaranteed $500 million to the RFC to be earmarked for loans to the states for public works. It signaled the acceptance of federal work relief projects as a depression palliative.

The Bonus Army

Hoover's opposition to work relief reinforced a widespread public image of him as a "heartless" president and the Bonus Army Riot in July confirmed that impression. The Bonus Army was composed of jobless veterans who had come to Washington from all over the country in quest of a bonus for their First World War service that Congress had promised them in 1924 for full payment in 1945. But the veterans demanded their compensation in 1932.

Beginning with a nucleus in Portland, Oregon, a "Bonus Expeditionary Force" of 300 veterans rode the rails until it reached East St Louis, Illinois. There it first attracted national attention by clashing with the Illinois National Guard, which had been called out to keep the "army" off the trains. Thereafter volunteer truckers whisked the group from state to state until it rolled into Washington on May 29 waving American flags, unfurling a banner that read, "Give Us a Bonus or Give Us a Job," and vowing to stay until 1945 if necessary. Thousands more unemployed veterans, some with their families, joined the BEF in the nation's capital until their numbers passed an estimated 20,000. They lobbied politely in Congress for their bonus, but to no avail. Hoover opposed paying the bonus as a threat to a balanced budget; Governor Franklin D. Roosevelt of New York endorsed that view. Many relief advocates in Congress pointed out that all the jobless needed relief and that it was unfair to single out any special group as more deserving than another. The House of Representatives approved the bonus but the Senate on June 17 rejected it while the veterans stood massed on the Capitol steps. A bugle sounded, they sang "America" and returned to their encampment on Anacostia Flats and elsewhere in Washington.

Most of them had no homes or jobs to return to. They lived in makeshift shanties, in pup tents supplied by the government, and in abandoned buildings due for demolition. Their food was doled out from relief organizations and the government. Many of them left Washington but thousands remained, living in unhealthy conditions, an ominous threat of disorder in the capital. Hoover sought appropriations to send them home but thousands refused to go. They lived by semimilitary discipline under factional leadership. The Washington police department treated them kindly, as did the administration in a quiet, unpublicized way. Everyone wanted them to leave, but the veterans stayed; the city was made uneasy by their presence.

On a hot day in late July the police attempted to move

Above: Members of the "Bonus Army," en route to Washington, DC, await transport in Illinois. Right: The morning after the demonstration: many men had slept in the Capitol's grounds overnight.

some veterans out of an abandoned building. The veterans resisted. In the melee two veterans were shot and killed by panicky policemen. The army was called in by the police and the secretary of war. Four troops of cavalry, four companies of infantry, six tanks, and a mounted machine gun squadron were placed under the command of General Douglas MacArthur. Major Dwight D. Eisenhower was his aide and another future general, George S. Patton, Jr was among his officers. Despite President Hoover's order not to attack the veterans, MacArthur moved in with gas and swords and burned their camp. More than 1,000 persons were gassed, 63 were injured and 135 were arrested. The expelled veterans were dispersed through the nation. Although Hoover had a good record on veterans' affairs and had unobtrusively aided the BEF, he justified MacArthur's assault as proof that "Government cannot be coerced by mob rule," and

characterized the BEF as a revolutionary Communist conspiracy.

The Bonus March, following Hoover's resistance to work relief, magnified his image as a heartless, cruel leader. Some of the bitterness it engendered is shown in this BEF parody:

Hoover is our shepherd

We are in want

He maketh us to lie

Down on the park benches

He leadeth us beside the still factories

He disturbeth our soul

He leadeth us in the path of destruction for his
   party's sake

Yea, though we walk through the valley of
   depression

We anticipate no recovery for those who art with us

Their politicians and diplomats frighten us

Thou preparest a reduction of our salary in the
   presence of our enemies

Our expenses runneth over

Surely poverty and unemployment will follow us

The Bonus Army's peaceful demonstration ended in rifle shots and flames. Left: General Douglas MacArthur, Major Dwight D. Eisenhower, and an officer carrying a gas mask watch army operations against the war veterans' camp at Anacostia Flats. Above: The Bonus Army encampment was set afire on MacArthur's orders.

> Through all the days of the Republican
>   Administration
> And we will dwell in mortgaged homes forever.

Hoover later claimed that the nation was experiencing recovery in mid-1932 and there is evidence to support him. Still, it is doubtful that Roosevelt's nomination was the reason for the deepening depression, as Hoover claimed. Hoover's leadership suffered from a conception of American society as the cooperative community it ought to be, rather than what it was. A shrewd organizer, administrator, and bureaucratic politician, Hoover was beaten by his unwillingness to violate his social and economic concepts or utilize political institutions. As president in any time he would have been a failure; but in the depression, Hoover was a disaster.

Chapter 2

NOTHING TO FEAR

"I pledge you, I pledge myself, to a new deal for the American people." Although these words of Franklin Delano Roosevelt at the Democratic Convention in 1932 promised a new era, few could have foreseen the far-reaching changes his presidency would usher in from March 1933. Despite the physical handicap under which he labored, Roosevelt fought an aggressive campaign, expanding on the need for "bold, persistent experimentation" to combat the depression. On taking office he plunged into the task of making capitalism work. From 1935 he came under increasing fire from political opponents skeptical of his motives, and battled a hostile Supreme Court. But Roosevelt persevered, introducing reforms that transformed the life of every American.

A Mandate for Recovery

Franklin Delano Roosevelt took office as president of the United States on March 4, 1933. He faced a country of 125 million people reeling under the impact of the worst economic crisis in American history—reeling, indeed, under a more severe political crisis than any since the outbreak of the Civil War seventy years before. By March 1933 the American economy had collapsed: at least 14 million out of a labor force of 52 million were unemployed. Compared with the 1923 average, industrial production was at 59 per cent, freight car loadings at 50 per cent, and factory payrolls were only 37 per cent of the earlier year. In thirty-six states banking operations had ceased and all exchanges were closed. But of the 14 million unemployed, only about a quarter were receiving any kind of social assistance. An observer in Chicago in 1932 reported: "Around the truck which was unloading garbage and other refuse were about 35 men, women and children. As soon as the truck pulled away from the pile, all started digging with sticks, some with their hands, grabbing bits of food and vegetables." In farming areas conditions were equally grim. In bitter weather on the great plains travelers would occasionally encounter a light blue haze that smelled like roasting coffee; many farmers were burning last year's corn to keep warm. The foodstuff was far cheaper at $1.40 a ton than coal which was already selling at $4.00 for the same amount.

On that same March 4, the American people heard over the still-novel invention of nationwide radio the new president take his oath of office to "protect, preserve, and defend the Constitution of the United States." They heard a rich and strong voice, vibrant with confidence, a voice to which they would become accustomed during the next twelve years of dramatic history. It was a voice made for radio, and which radio made familiar to all Americans. Franklin Roosevelt's first inaugural speech was one of the greatest in American history. It was a reassertion of faith and courage and of belief in the ability of the American people to solve their problems through democratic processes. "The only thing we have to fear," he stated, "is fear itself—nameless, unreasoning, unjustified terror which paralyzes needed efforts to convert retreat into advance." In a time of near-universal panic, a man unafraid had assumed command.

Nothing here should have surprised the American people, for the spirit of daring, the readiness to accept responsibility and, once accepted, to enjoy it, had marked the man's political campaign. That campaign had been fought over the causes and the possible remedies for the Great Depression. His predecessor, Herbert Hoover, had believed that the American economy was fundamentally sound, but that it had been disturbed by the repercussions of a worldwide depression, the causes of which could be traced back to the First World War. Behind this argument lay the clear implication that Hoover would prefer to depend on the natural processes of recovery, while FDR wished to use the authority of the federal government for bold remedial experiments. The election gave Roosevelt a clear victory of 22.8 million votes to Hoover's 15.7 million.

Yet Hoover was no mere stand-patter. There are those who see him, in fact, as the real father of the New Deal. But there was a clear difference in spirit and, as events were to prove, in the scale of FDR's policies. Republicans claimed that there was some evidence as early as the spring of 1932 that business was beginning to recover and that this recovery was interrupted by the presidential campaign and its outcome. They claimed, with some justice, that the further decline of business in the winter of 1932–33 was due to Roosevelt's failure to commit himself publicly to Hoover's policies of a balanced budget, government economy, and sound money.

The country suffered acutely from the lame-duck situation that prevailed at the time. A president elected in November did not take office until the following March. In this long interregnum the economy deteriorated, and Roosevelt refused all Hoover's approaches to him to concert their policies. Whether the crisis was actually the result of Hoover's hesitations or of Roosevelt's refusal to commit himself is an open question. But it undoubtedly deepened in the four-month period when both president and president-elect were in effect powerless. This situation was changed when the Twentieth or Lame-duck Amendment to the Constitution was ratified in 1933. The inauguration date was moved up to January 20 and the newly elected Congress now convened in January instead of the December following the elections.

It was FDR's courage that was the striking feature not only of his campaign, but his life; a courage that was itself a product of his own remarkable personal history. He was born with a silver spoon in his mouth, on January 30, 1882. Despite his Dutch name, he was mainly English by blood, with several pilgrim fathers among his ancestors. He seemed from the start to be destined to be one of fortune's darlings, and indeed his early reputation was that of a lightweight. With wealth and a long family tradition behind him, he did not have to struggle to arrive. He was an only and a spoiled child; when he went on from Groton school to Harvard, his mother Sara accompanied him, both doting and domineering.

His father, who was president or vice-president of

Roosevelt's inaugural address dramatically foreshadowed a new course for the United States. The president's nationally broadcast statement on March 4, 1933, brought hope and cheer to a disheartened nation.

various railway companies, owned a large estate, Hyde Park, on the Hudson sixty miles from New York, where he interested himself in cattle breeding and lived the life of a country gentleman. He died in December 1900, just after Franklin entered Harvard. To the young man Hyde Park was always home, and his permanent political base. He grew up tall and strikingly handsome, sporting, athletic, and with easy and charming manners. He had a passion for the sea and wanted in fact to enter the Navy. Neither at school nor university did he show any special scholastic flair. His major achievement was to get on to the staff of the Harvard *Crimson* and to scoop an interview with the college president. In 1905, while he was still at Columbia Law School, he married his distant cousin, Anna Eleanor Roosevelt. He had apparently fallen in love with her when she was still a gawky schoolgirl. Two years later he was admitted to the bar and joined a firm of New York lawyers. At his country home he was a genial host and squire; a life of ease, elegance, and affluence apparently lay before him.

In 1910 he was persuaded to run for the New York State Senate as a Democrat in what seemed to be a hopelessly Republican constituency on the Hudson River. To his own and his friends' surprise he won the election, and moved with his wife and three young children to Albany to begin his political career. In 1913 under Democrat Woodrow Wilson, he became assistant-secretary of the navy, a post held sixteen years earlier by his fifth cousin Theodore Roosevelt, in whose long and friendly shadow his own career was being cast. He retained the office for eight years. In Washington he learned the politics of the Democratic party and became interested in foreign affairs, traveling to Britain and the European battle zones. FDR was the running mate of Governor James M. Cox of Ohio in the presidential election of 1920 in which they unsuccessfully argued in favor of the League of Nations. Most characteristic of his career was his constant and apparently easy success. But it had come less by work than by contact; by the fact that both his birth and natural gifts started him high up on the ladder. His ability had been proved, but not as yet his character.

In 1921, while vacationing at his summer home on Campobello Island just off the Maine coast in New Brunswick, Franklin Roosevelt contracted polio. He was thirty-nine years old, and from this time on paralyzed from the waist down. He spent the next few years on his back learning, if nothing else, infinite patience and acquiring a deep sympathy for suffering of any kind. This gave him an inner feeling of security and self-confidence; he thought he could overcome all his handicaps through sheer willpower and the desire to conquer. He became an active swimmer, notably at Warm Springs, Georgia, and learned to walk again with leg braces. He was later to buy the Springs and develop them as a charitable

Eleanor Roosevelt was the most politically active First Lady in the nation's history. Her work continued long after FDR's death; Douglas Chandor's painting shows her in 1949.

facility for the treatment of infantile paralysis.

Roosevelt's illness brought him a group of dedicated friends: Louis Howe, Harry Hopkins, Robert Sherwood, Archibald MacLeish; the latter two became his brilliant speech writers. Mrs Roosevelt learned not only to be his nurse but also his political eyes and ears, a roving correspondent on his behalf, and a journalist and personality in her own right. She was to become the self-appointed conscience of his administration.

One very striking feature of Roosevelt's subsequent life was the discretion with which his physical incapacity was treated by the press and by radio commentators. He was rarely if ever photographed in motion. The public usually only saw his strong upper torso; they never saw him struggling to walk, hunched over, two canes in hand with a man at each arm. In simple fact the man who was elected to the presidency four times could not walk. But as Al Smith said in 1928, "A governor doesn't have to be an acrobat."

The lessons polio brought FDR were not immediately discernible. His public reputation until his illness was that of a lightweight. To Edmund Wilson, the critic and writer, he was "a politically immature boy scout." When it was first suggested to his old friend and mentor Al Smith, that FDR should run for the governorship of New York, Smith barked, "Out of the question! You know as well as I do that Frank hasn't any brains."

FDR's Rise to Leadership

But on June 26, 1924 it was that same Frank who proposed Al Smith for the presidential nomination at Madison Square Garden in New York. It was the only speech of consequence that Roosevelt made in the whole seven years of his convalescence. FDR was on crutches, but there was nothing wrong with his voice or his enthusiasm. He talked for thirty-four minutes and when he termed his man "the happy warrior of the political battlefield," there was an incredible eruption of enthusiasm which lasted for seventy-three minutes. Smith did not get the nomination, but the New York *World* wrote

that no matter what happened to Smith, FDR would stand out as the real hero of the event. "Adversity has lifted him above the bickering, the religious bigotry, the conflicting personal ambitions and petty sectional prejudices . . . it has made him the one leader commanding the respect and admiration of delegations from all sections of the land." When Al Smith was nominated for the presidency four years later and had to give up the governorship of New York, he persuaded Roosevelt, much against his will, to accept the Democratic nomination for the governorship. FDR would rather have waited. His physical recovery was not complete and 1928 was not likely to be a good year for the Democrats. But he did run and won, while Hoover defeated Smith. Smith never got over this and fell out with Roosevelt over patronage, remaining to the end a bitter critic of his former ally.

The press and the public had recognized Roosevelt's

FDR leans on his crutches in this rare 1924 photograph revealing his disability. He is speaking to John W. Davies, and the governor of New York, Al Smith (holding cigar).

The Democrats' promise to repeal prohibition was given as much prominence as the candidates themselves on this bumper plate. John Nance Garner was Roosevelt's vice-presidential running mate in 1932.

suffering and resultant maturity. Historian Will Durant had seen and recorded FDR nominating Smith at the Democratic convention of 1928 in Houston, Texas:

> Here on the stage is Franklin Roosevelt, beyond comparison the finest man that has appeared at either convention; beside him the master minds who held the platform at Kansas City were crude bourgeois, porters suddenly made rich.
>
> A figure tall and proud even in suffering; a face of classic profile; pale with years of struggle against paralysis; a frame nervous and yet self-controlled with that tense, taut unity of spirit which lifts the complex soul above those whose calmness is only a stolidity; most obviously a gentleman and a scholar. A man softened and cleansed and illumined with pain. What in the name of Croker and Tweed is he doing here? . . .
>
> Hear the nominating speech; it is not a battery of rockets, bombs and tear-drawing gas—it is not shouted, it is quietly read; there is hardly a gesture, hardly a raising of the voice. This is a civilized man. . . . For the moment we are lifted up.

Roosevelt settled into the governorship of New York quickly. Moreover he had a good record as governor, carrying on a program (started by Smith) of slow, cautious, liberal reform. The program included old-age pensions, unemployment insurance, protective legislation for women and children in industry, an improved employment service, state-owned electric utilities, and a 100 per cent increase in the income tax. All this was achieved despite the dominance in the state legislature of corrupt Tammany politicians and conservative figures from upstate New York. James Farley, the boxing commissioner of New York and chairman of the state Democratic committee, stated after Roosevelt's reelection in 1930 that he did not see how Roosevelt could escape being the Democratic presidential candidate in 1932, even if no one were to lift a finger on behalf of his candidacy.

Farley himself began to lift a finger immediately; he made tours through most of the states, carrying Roosevelt's cause to the grass-roots Democratic political organization. He found increasingly that party leaders were beginning to think of Roosevelt as the one man who could lead them to victory in 1932. They cared little what his principles were (very likely, Roosevelt himself was not certain what policies he would follow if he were to become president); they were willing to support him simply because he looked a winner. When the Republican convention met in Chicago in June 1932 its delegates were far from happy. The Democrats had already won a victory in the off-year elections of 1930 and the depression was steadily worsening. The delegates duly went on to renominate Hoover and Charles Curtis.

When the Democrats, in turn, moved into Chicago they knew that the odds for victory were with them. Their platform was little different from that of the Republicans. It called for austerity and a balanced budget, taxation based on the ability to pay, and a few minor economic reforms. But in two matters it did strike a different note: it favored a reduction of tariff, and an outright repeal of the Eighteenth (Prohibition) Amendment. Among the obvious candidates were John Nance Garner of Texas, Speaker of the House since 1931, Al Smith, strongly backed by the Scripps-Howard newspaper chain, and Newton D. Baker, Woodrow Wilson's secretary of war. But from the start the odds were on Roosevelt. He had not only won the governorship of New York against the tide in 1928, he had been reelected in 1930 by a greatly increased majority.

In a speech made in Georgia a month before the convention, Roosevelt had declared that the country needed and demanded "bold, persistent experimentation," and that it was only common sense to try one method and then, if that failed, another. "But above all," he urged, the government had to "try something." This promise to take firm action, however imprecise, made a strong impact on the American people.

Roosevelt had a clear majority on the first ballot at the Democratic convention, but not the necessary two-thirds vote. He gained slightly in the second and third ballots, but Farley began to fear that the delegates would bolt to a dark-horse candidate. He also saw that the large bloc of Smith votes in the eastern states could not possibly be won over. Roosevelt's one chance lay in acquiring the Garner delegates from Texas and California. Consequently, after adjournment following the third ballot, he telephoned William Randolph Hearst, who was the ultimate power behind the Garner forces. Hearst was warned that the alternatives to FDR would very likely be either a dark-horse candidate like Newton D. Baker—who was a Wilsonian idealist and internationalist—or even worse (in Hearst's eyes) Al Smith. Hearst soon agreed to release the Garner delegates to Roosevelt, provided that Garner be given the vice-presidential nomination. All the other delegates, with the exception of the irreconcilable Smith forces, proceeded to get on the Roosevelt bandwagon. True to Farley's promise, Garner was given the vice-presidential nomination.

Franklin Roosevelt campaigns for the presidency from the back seat of his touring car in Elm Grove, West Virginia, in 1932. His dynamic enthusiasm captured the imagination of voters.

UPI

Roosevelt immediately flew to Chicago to accept the nomination in person. He took with him a fighting speech drawn up for him by a group of advisers, who came to be known collectively as the Brain Trust, including Raymond Moley, Rexford Tugwell, and Adolf Berle, Jr. At the Chicago airport his political secretary, Louis Howe, handed him a second speech. Having no time to compare the two speeches, Roosevelt shuffled their pages about as he stood on the platform acknowledging the enthusiastic greeting, and characteristically proceeded to read the first page of Howe's speech and then to switch to the Brain Trust speech, which he read in its entirety.

It was in this speech that Roosevelt announced: "I pledge you, I pledge myself, to a new deal for the American people. . . . Give me your help, not to win votes alone, but to win in this crusade to restore America to its own people." His proposed measures were specific but contradictory. Unemployment relief and social security were promised, as well as a policy of government economy and balancing the budget; but also included were soil conservation and reforestation, federal regulation of security exchanges and holding companies, the development of publicly owned electric power, and not least "a continuous responsibility of government for human welfare."

Hoover's campaign was quiet and dignified—and utterly ineffectual. It was marred by the invasion of Washington by the "Bonus Army" and its subsequent forcible expulsion by the army. It was further weakened by the defection of a group of progressive Republicans to Roosevelt including George Norris, Bob La Follette, and Hiram Johnson. Roosevelt's own campaign was militant, vigorous, contradictory—and jovial. The song "Happy Days Are Here Again" followed him everywhere. The campaign was also very successful—only six states outside New England gave their votes to Hoover.

The New President and the New Deal

When the president took office on March 4 the crisis was already upon the American people. Banks had already been closed in all the larger states, and on March 5 a presidential proclamation ordered a nation-wide bank holiday. Various government agencies, including the Treasury Department and the Federal Reserve Board, attempted to investigate the financial condition of each bank and determine quickly the degree of solvency. Those banks which were found to be sound would be allowed to reopen; those which were not would stay closed. This first act of Roosevelt's met with approval from the whole country, and especially from the nation's bankers. Congress was called into special session on March 9. By the evening of that day, in a record-breaking

feat of speed, both houses had organized, formed committees, and passed the emergency banking legislation the draft of which they had received from the administration only ten hours earlier. This legislation authorized the president to take the actions already begun by executive order. The government was permitted to issue emergency currency.

On Sunday, March 12, Roosevelt went before the people in his first "fireside chat" over the radio. In the informal, easy manner which was to characterize these "chats," he explained exactly what the new bank policy would be. He assured the people that those banks which were found to be sound would be allowed to reopen.

On March 13 the "sound banks" (with 90 per cent of the nation's deposits) were permitted to reopen. A policy of moderate currency inflation was launched in order to start an upward movement in commodity prices and to afford some relief to debtors. More generous credit facilities were made available through new governmental agencies. Savings bank deposits up to $5,000 were insured, and severe regulations imposed on the manner in which securities could be sold on the stock exchange. There was no economic theory or broad principle involved in this series of successful moves. Simply by taking positive, constructive action, Roosevelt had restored public confidence and thus rescued the banking system. It was essentially a conservative action; its only radical aspect was the speed with which it had been executed. On March 5, Roosevelt had had the opportunity to demand the complete nationalization of the banks, and Congress probably would have supported him. But Roosevelt acted to save the banking structure without any drastic or major reform of it. Raymond Moley later observed that if there was ever any moment when things hung in the balance, it was March 5, 1933; capitalism in the United States, he said, was saved by Franklin D. Roosevelt in a period of eight days.

The president, noticeably reluctant and apparently bewildered in the four months between November and March, now moved fast. He clearly was his own man. In the congressional session from March 9 to June 16, the "Hundred Days," Congress passed an enormous number of measures. The emphasis was on relief legislation as a preliminary to recovery, but what was striking was the method and the style as well as the speed and the content. The legislation would be drawn up by the administration—in large part by the Brain Trust—and then sent to Congress for approval in skeletal form. It was considered that there was no time to work out the remedies for any given emergency in detail. In this way Congress was giving to the president an unprecedented authority. Farley, now postmaster general, kept a careful record of how each Democratic senator and congressman voted on each measure. Congressional leaders were regularly in conference with the Brain Trust or with the

By the time Collier's *appeared in the administration's first week, FDR had already dealt successfully with a grave bank crisis. Roosevelt's cabinet included (clockwise) Frances Perkins as secretary of labor, Henry Morgenthau, Jr as secretary of the Treasury, and Harold Ickes in the department of the interior. Rexford Tugwell (bottom right) advised the president from the White House.*

president himself, agreeing on necessary compromises.

The initiative clearly lay with the man in the White House and his team. And his team included an impressive if unorthodox cabinet. As secretary of the Treasury, the president first chose William Woodin, but he took ill in 1934 and was then replaced by Henry Morgenthau, a firm New Dealer. Cordell Hull, the veteran congressman from Tennessee and ardent low-tariff advocate, took over the department of state. The department of the interior went to Harold Ickes, the contentious and aggressive Bull Mooser who became and stayed a friend of Roosevelt through the years. Frances Perkins, the first woman to hold a cabinet office, was secretary of labor, and Henry Wallace, whose father had held the same post in both the Harding and Coolidge administrations, was secretary of agriculture. In the background and on the sidelines stood the Brain Trust with Rex Tugwell, Judge Sammy Rosenman (Sammy the Rose), Adolf Berle, and Raymond Moley from Columbia University.

The emphasis of the Hundred Days legislation was less on reform than on relief and recovery. After the economic crisis had deepened so seriously in the spring of 1933, the Roosevelt administration abandoned its campaign promises of government economy and a balanced budget, and engaged in a program of deficit financing in order to provide federal relief. Roosevelt did not believe that relief was the province of private charity, as did Hoover, but rather a matter of society's duty since the depression was a social rather than an individual failing.

Under the New Deal, a new agency, the Federal Emergency Relief Administration, provided relief funds to the states in the form of outright grants. By 1935, over $4 billion had been granted for purposes of direct relief, and by 1940 the sum had reached $16 billion. To Roosevelt, however, a "dole" was not enough. That would serve to keep the unemployed in existence but it would not get them back to productive work. The president's idea of relief was to provide employment that permanently added to the country's wealth, and he wanted the ensuing recovery to be on a healthier basis than the feverish boom which had followed the recession of the early 1920s.

A second relief measure, the Civilian Conservation Corps, was designed to take young unemployed men, between the ages of 17 and 25, off the labor market and send them to camps where they would do healthful work on conservation projects. The CCC reduced unemployment pressure, provided relief, injected more purchasing power into the economy as a whole (since the families of the young men received $25 out of the usual $30 monthly pay), and conserved and increased the natural resources of the country. Three million young people passed through the 2,600 camps of the CCC in eight years. They constructed roads and landing fields, and worked on fire prevention, soil erosion, and flood control projects. Because the program was at least a partial answer to the delinquency problem, and because it created more national wealth than it consumed, the CCC became one of the most consistently popular of the New Deal programs. Roosevelt must be given the credit for the agency, since he conceived the idea and formulated it in legislation.

Harry Hopkins was placed in charge of the new Civil Works Administration in November 1933. It provided relief work for over 4 million people and spent more than $1 billion. New Dealers believed that where possible it was better to provide relief by works projects rather than by the laying out of a cash dole. By converting funds into wages and short-term projects, rather than into materials and equipment, the CWA was able to "prime the pump" of the economy efficiently.

The program was remarkable in containing a provision for artists. Roosevelt himself developed the idea that unemployed artists should be put to work at something which they could do and like to do, and decided that there must be public places where paintings were wanted. This was part of the whole general idea behind the CWA— that the program should be fitted into the particular talents, needs and desires of each individual.

All of these measures could be described as primarily relief programs. Another new program, the Public Works Administration, was designed not only to provide relief but to promote recovery. Three billion dollars were appropriated for the program under Harold Ickes, the honest, blustering secretary of the interior. By 1936, the PWA could take credit for 1,497 water works, 883 sewage plants, 741 highway improvements, 263 hospitals, 166 bridges, and 70 municipal power plants. Over $500 million had been spent on school buildings. Under its auspices, artists were commissioned to paint murals in the public buildings; writers assigned to publicize the government's programs; and musicians formed into touring orchestras to bring music to the countryside. One of the most impressive byproducts of the New Deal was its stimulus to writers, artists, and sculptors. The Federal Writers Project produced over a thousand publications, including fifty-one state guides—a remarkable achieve-

*Top left: A song sheet sounds the praises of
the NRA. Top: After their first day at Camp Dix,
New Jersey, youthful enlistees cheer the CCC.
Elsewhere, workers installed curbstones (left)
for the WPA in New York City and the Federal
Music Project (above) prepared for an outdoor
performance of Aida in California.*

ment according to the historian William Leuchtenberg:

> The 150 volumes in the "Life in America" series ranged from the moving *These are Our Lives* to *Baseball in Old Chicago* and embraced a notable series of ethnic studies, including *The Italians of New York, The Hopi, The Armenians of Massachusetts,* and *The Negro in Virginia*. The projects . . . reflected the fascination of the thirties with the rediscovery of regional lore, the delighted recapture of place names—Corncake Inlet, Money Island, Frying Pan Shoals—and the retelling of long forgotten tales of Indian raids. The project made use of the talents of established writers such as Conrad Aiken, who wrote the description of Deerfield for the Massachusetts state guide, and new men like John Cheever and Richard Wright. . . . Commercial publishers were happy to print most of the guides, and many of them sold exceptionally well.

By 1939 it could be claimed that Public Works projects had been instituted in all but three counties of the United States. There was a remarkable freedom from graft and corruption. Despite the vast sums passing through innumerable hands, FDR could proudly boast that the New Deal had "no Teapot Dome."

The first New Deal—the heavy legislative program of the years from 1933 to 1935—concerned itself with currency reform, providing an economic stimulus, and with basic reforms in agriculture and industry. The Glass-Steagall Banking Act of 1933 was designed to prevent the future collapse of the private banking system. Its most popular provision created the Federal Deposit Insurance Corporation (FDIC) to insure all deposits up to $5,000. The "Truth in Securities" Act (1933) required that all securities offered for sale in interstate commerce be exactly what they were purported to be. By the Securities Exchange Act (1934) stock exchanges were regulated and licensed under the Securities and Exchange Commission.

In April 1933, the United States went off the gold standard, and a month later the president was authorized to inflate the currency by adding $3 billion in new treasury notes, or by reducing the gold content of the dollar up to 50 per cent. The government also began purchasing gold at high prices, seeking to devalue the dollar still further. The financial measures did not succeed in raising prices, while security holders lost heavily. But foreign trade was stimulated by the dollar devaluation, which lowered the price of American goods abroad.

Hoover's Reconstruction Finance Corporation was given new powers in 1934 in an attempt to encourage private enterprise. It was authorized to grant loans ($11 billion before 1936) to industries as well as to railroads and banks. The housing situation in 1933 was bleak. Not only had home building shrunk to a negligible point, but many homeowners were unable to keep up their mortgage payments. Congress passed measures to remedy this state of affairs. The Home Owners Loan Corporation (1933) loaned money to mortgage holders faced with the loss of their property; the HOLC saved the homes of over 1 million Americans. The Federal Housing Administration (1934) was empowered to insure mortgages issued by private concerns for construction purposes.

To stimulate industry, the National Industrial Recovery Act was passed; it set up the National Recovery Administration (NRA), headed by the fiery General Hugh Johnson. This program was neither a happy nor a successful experiment in the control of production. The general was prompt to attack "chiselers and eye-gouging and ear-chewing in business." Whatever spirit of cooperation was bred under the Blue Eagle symbol was largely destroyed by his impetuosity and gruffness. He was persuaded to resign after a year in office. The agency initials, said the disenchanted, stood for "No Recovery Allowed." The whole experiment was eventually declared unconstitutional.

The Roosevelt program of agricultural recovery rested on two foundations: easing the debt burden of the farmer and raising prices through crop control. The Farm Credit Administration refinanced farm mortgages at low rates, advanced money for current needs, and bought back foreclosed property. By 1936 the FCA had lent $3.7 billion. Under the Agricultural Adjustment Act (1933) farmers who agreed to restrict their output were compensated out of money raised from taxing processors. Farmers plowed under countless acres of cotton and wheat, killed millions of pigs, and destroyed part of the tobacco crop. The program, said historian Richard Hofstadter, represented "organized scarcity in action." Farm crop prices rose rapidly, and thanks to higher prices and benefit payments, the farmers' cash income rose from $4.3 billion in 1927 to $7 billion in 1935. City dwellers complained of the rising cost of food, so the New Deal created the Federal Commodities Corporation (1933) which distributed surplus food among welfare recipients.

The Tennessee Valley Authority was the most ambitious of all the president's schemes. The valley of the great Tennessee River covered some 40,000 square miles, and parts of seven different states. It had immense economic and farming possibilities which had not been realized because the area was comparatively poor and backward. A majestic river, with tremendous water power, was running to waste just because it had never been harnessed to the making of electrical power. The full development of the valley would need large amounts of capital, and the president determined that the government, not private capitalists, should undertake it. Roosevelt meant to build not just the economic but the social prosperity of the valley dwellers—with which, he held, private capitalism would not much concern itself. The whole attempt was remarkable, because it was not just a case of government

Brown Brothers

*Georgia cotton is plowed under for the new
Agricultural Adjustment Administration in 1933.
Production was restricted by destroying standing
crops and removing land from cultivation in
order to raise farm prices.*

going into business—itself a complete reversal of Hoover-Republican ideas—but a case of the national government embarking upon planned economy. Considering how completely capitalist is the American mind, Roosevelt's scheme becomes all the more remarkable. It turned out to be a great success, but it was a real gamble. If it had failed, the "rugged individualists," who took a very poor view of the president's interference in business, would have claimed the failure as proof that only "individual enterprise" could successfully tackle a big economic development.

The Muscle Shoals Act of 1933 created the Tennessee Valley Authority. Power was granted to build dams on the river, convert the water power into electricity, and then distribute it to the valley's inhabitants. It could also regulate agriculture, provide fertilizers and other necessities, make provision for flood control, rehouse the rural population, provide educational and recreational amenities, and in general "advance the economic and social well-being of the people living in the said river basin." A whole series of huge dams and hydroelectric plants was built by the TVA, improving the navigation of the river and supplying the cheap electricity to an average of one in every seven farms. Formerly, only one farm out of every thirteen had enjoyed electric power. This was supplied by private companies, which now had to bring down their prices to meet the government's competition. Since these power companies had a capital of $12 million tied up in their plants, they grew very angry with Roosevelt. But in a test case in 1936 the Supreme Court upheld the government's right to be in the power business. By 1941 the TVA was supplying cheap electricity to 400,000 customers. Indeed, so successful was the government in raising the whole standard of living in the region that a similar scheme was undertaken in the far Northwest, in the Columbia River basin. The building of the Grand Coulee (1933) and Bonneville (1937) dams made irrigation possible on such a scale that more than a million acres of desert could be reclaimed for agriculture; the dams also provided vast amounts of cheap electricity.

Assessing the Early Years

How successful then was the first New Deal in bringing about relief and recovery? If it was a "program," it contained many internal contradictions. Some measures were inflationary, others were deflationary. To achieve economies, salaries of government workers were cut by 25 per cent in the first weeks of the New Deal; there were also severe cuts in veterans' payments. But the devaluation of the currency and deficit financing were clearly inflationary in tendency. As it concerned the farmers, the New Deal was based on an economy of scarcity, but plainly the philosophy of the TVA and PWA was that of an economics of abundance. In the NRA and the AAA there was an artificial restriction on production and monopolistic conditions were accepted; at the same time, monopoly was curbed by the SEC. The New Deal can perhaps best be described as in fact a system of national economics, almost of national socialism. In its first two years FDR all but totally ignored the outside world and was ready to be cold and indifferent to its problems. The New Deal was applauded by the economist J. M. Keynes, even though FDR and Keynes did not understand each other when they met in 1934. It would have been applauded by Hitler if he had understood it. Part of the recovery was due to deliberate planning; part was due to enormous public spending and subsidies; part was due to a prodding of industry which it would be flattering to call direction. But the objective was not philosophic consistency but urgent relief and recovery.

The most important acts were those aimed at the recovery not only of the capitalist but of the democratic system—the steps taken to meet the bank crisis in the first weeks, the manipulation of the currency, the NRA, the AAA, the PWA. Behind the efforts to achieve economic recovery lay the recognition of the obligation on the federal government to grant relief to the unemployed and to the needy in the form of cash payments or employment on work projects. In the first two years the measures for reform, like the SEC, the FDIC, and the TVA, were seen as of lesser importance. The central purpose was to keep the people and the economy surviving until the confidence that prices were steadily rising and that investments were safe would cause industry to revive. To assist in this process consumers were to be given sufficient purchasing power to buy the surplus products of industry and agriculture. FDR was extremely unpopular with

Dams were constructed for electric power, flood control, and irrigation as in the Muscle Shoals project of the TVA (top) and at Grand Coulee in Washington (left). The inset shows a panel from Construction of the Dam *by William Gropper.*

capitalists, yet his goal was simply to save the capitalist system from collapse and to do so by refusing to balance the books.

His enemies, and there were many of them, bitterly detested "that man in the White House." As he put it, with a customary grin, "Everybody is against me—except the electorate." In fact, the first New Deal was essentially conservative. At no point in his entire first program, with the possible exception of the TVA, did the president have the intention of altering the basic economic system under which the country was governed. The banks were reopened under their own management and ownership although the president could easily have carried through a full-scale program of nationalization. The AAA and the NRA, based as they were on raising prices by restricting production, were close to the heart of conservative big business. Even the great increase in deficit financing which bore the burden of the New Deal was a middle course between the followers of John Maynard Keynes, the brilliant British economist, and the president's own views. The "Keynesians" urged greater spending while FDR was reluctant to abandon the economic beliefs of a lifetime.

Roosevelt was a remarkable person. Arthur Schlesinger, Jr, said that he "cared for the people, battled for them and exulted in the battle." Harry Hopkins told Robert Sherwood, "You and I are for Roosevelt because he is a great spiritual figure, because he is an idealist." It is true that this quality in the man inspired the loyal service that so many men and women gave him. For his part he came to tantalize, to deceive, and to disappoint them. He could be ruthless even with his friends. But the Roosevelt of the New Deal was a more democratic and perhaps greater figure than the Roosevelt of the Second World War. Many people in many classes benefited from him. He forged an unusual alliance of the big cities and the countryside, the poor—black and white—and the not-so-poor, the South and the North. He gave them success and a cause, if not a creed. Some of his supporters backed him not because of his policies but because of the enemies he had made: from the beginning there were those behind the New Deal who were hostile to the trusts, to the monopolists, to the money-changers in the temple, to the economic royalists. But more than all this FDR gave Washington, and the country, faith in itself. The city was transformed from a placid and leisurely southern town into a breezy, sophisticated and metropolitan center. "Come at once to Washington," Senator La Follette, son of "Fighting Bob," telegraphed to Donald Richberg, the Progressive of twenty years before; "Great things are under way." And Norman Davis, who had known the president when he was the debonair young assistant-secretary of the navy, met a mutual friend on the White House steps. He said to him, "That fellow in there is not the fellow we used to know. There's been a miracle here."

Challenges to the New Deal

From 1935 to 1937, Franklin Roosevelt faced major challenges to his New Deal from many directions—from radicals and conservatives, from the Republican party, and from the United States Supreme Court. In this complex situation, Roosevelt made significant changes in his program in 1935 and 1936 and moved on to a spectacular victory over his Republican foes and his critics on the Right and Left. He did suffer his first major defeat when he attempted to reform the Supreme Court the following year, but even here he made a gain of sorts as the Court became more tolerant in its attitude toward the New Deal.

Roosevelt was a masterful politician operating in a difficult situation. He did not discard the two fundamental features of the early New Deal; the commitment to capitalism and confidence in federal action. But the administration became more critical of business leaders, more directly and actively concerned with the welfare of lower-income groups, and more interested in the growth of the labor movement.

One of the many factors which combined to move policies along these lines was the unsatisfactory rate of recovery from the depression. More than 10 million Americans still could not find jobs in spite of the strenuous efforts by government officials in 1933–34. Had the economy recovered more rapidly, Roosevelt could have ignored or at least paid less attention to his critics (and there would not have been so many of them). Instead, he was alarmed by them. He feared that without bold solutions, discontent and radical feeling would grow into a serious challenge to the American political and economic system—and to his position. Criticism from business leaders made him wary. Most of all, it strengthened Roosevelt's doubts about the wisdom of the businessmen, who did not seem to recognize the dangers that surrounded them. He was not encouraged to follow their advice for less government action when they did not seem wise enough to save themselves.

The congressional elections of 1934 also affected the president's thinking. They suggested quite clearly that the people wanted more help from government, not less. Roosevelt believed that acceptance of demands for cuts in government activities would defy the will of the people and might lead to his defeat in the 1936 elections. By 1935 Roosevelt faced strong pressures from different directions for change in his policies. From the Right came demands that the administration cut back on government activities and develop a more friendly attitude toward business. On

Jobless men form part of the daily line outside the state unemployment office in Memphis, Tennessee. Despite the New Deal efforts there were still 10 million unemployed in 1935.

Above: Norman Thomas raises a clenched fist and sings out lustily in celebration of his nomination as Socialist candidate in the 1936 elections. Thomas, who was the party's nominee for six successive campaigns until 1948, was as outspoken against communism as fascism.

the Left, various groups and individuals insisted that FDR expand the role of government and use it more effectively against the problems of lower-income people.

Late in the summer of 1934, a new political organization, called the Liberty League, had been formed. It brought together from both parties some prominent businessmen and politicians who disliked the New Deal. A well financed body, the Liberty League quickly became the principal mouthpiece for anti-New Deal conservatism.

Liberty Leaguers maintained that a revolution was taking place in America. The United States was rapidly becoming a very different kind of country; instead of the free nation it had been for generations, it was assuming the character of an absolute kingdom or a European totalitarian regime. The changes, these critics argued, were destroying "business confidence." The expectation that the future would be profitable must be restored. Without it, the nation could not recover from the depression. The New Deal was also destroying the character of the American people, the spirit of independence and enterprise that had made the nation great. The nation, the conservatives insisted, must return to the practices of the past and restore power to those who had

a more receptive attitude toward businessmen and their needs and beliefs.

Once, Roosevelt had appeared to be the defender of the American system, including American business; now, he seemed to the Liberty Leaguers to be the most serious threat to it. The leaguers held the conservative political views long endorsed by businessmen. They functioned as pressure groups had for years and sought to persuade the American people to select new leadership. Although their ideas and ways of behaving were old, the situation in which they found themselves was quite new. Business leaders had once been the major promoters of change in America, while others like the Populists and the Progressives had protested against them; now, the national government had become the chief impulse for change, and they objected.

On the Left of the political spectrum, the call for accel-

Both pictures: AP

Father Charles Coughlin (above left), the "radio priest," went from anti-Wall Street to pro-Fascist before being silenced by the church. Upton Sinclair (above), a utopian Socialist, ran as a Democrat in a bitter California gubernatorial contest in 1934.

eration of the pace of change came from many different individuals, united only by their sense of the inadequacies of the New Deal. One of the most prominent critics was Norman Thomas, the leader of the Socialist party in the United States. He insisted, above all, that the New Deal was not socialism and maintained instead that it was a misguided and haphazard effort to save capitalism and seemed likely to lead to fascism of the sort developing in Italy and Germany. He also attacked defects in specific programs, such as the eviction of sharecroppers in the South that accompanied the cuts in the production of cotton.

Other critics, with less systematic intellectual positions, gained even more support than Thomas. One of these was a Catholic priest from suburban Detroit, Father Charles Coughlin, who gained a broad and diverse following among Catholics in the East and Protestants in the Middle West. His radio broadcasts, which by 1934 featured attacks upon Roosevelt and the New Deal, charged that the president and his policies were dominated by the "international bankers" and called for major changes in the banking and money systems.

A Democratic senator from Louisiana, Huey Long, occupied an equally prominent position in the politics of 1934–35. Like Coughlin, Long had supported Roosevelt at first but had grown dissatisfied and soon found support for his criticism in many parts of the country. By 1935, Long was denouncing Roosevelt as a captive of big business. Long led a new political organization, the "Share Our Wealth Society," advocating a redistribution of wealth in the United States that would favor the poorer people, and alarming Democratic leaders with plans for a campaign for the presidency.

Thomas, Coughlin, and Long were but three of the most prominent radicals in the period. The list also included men such as Upton Sinclair who ran for governor of California in 1934. End Poverty in California (EPIC) was his slogan and symbol. Also in California, Dr Francis E. Townsend rallied old people in a crusade for large pensions. Under the Townsend plan, the government would give every unemployed person over sixty $200 a

The Louisiana Kingfish

Government by the landed rich or the city corrupt was Louisiana tradition when Huey Long struggled and pushed his way to the state's highest office and then toward the US presidency in the early 1930s. He had maintained a remarkable pace for a poor farm boy by half-working and half-talking his way through law school in only eight months and being elected to a public utilities board before he was twenty-five. As commissioner he had dramatically turned the board into an agent of reform by successfully challenging the oil and telephone monopolies.

Success also meant there were numerous attempts to divert the young crusader from the power he had so obviously begun to covet. But Huey Long was nothing if not politically agile. He outsmarted worried Baton Rouge politicians even when they charged him with nineteen offences ranging from cursing to corruption to hiring a man named Battling Bozeman to assassinate a legislator. As Long himself once pointed out, "There may be smarter guys than Huey Long but they ain't in Louisiana."

Long brought his country ways, and

showmanship, to the governor's mansion in 1928. "What Huey did, in effect," wrote journalist Hamilton Basso, "was to stride into the governor's office, take off his coat, put his feet on the desk, and spit tobacco juice on the walls." Just being himself, he created an international incident by receiving the commander of a German cruiser in his pajamas. After one disappointing Louisiana State football game, he tried unsuccessfully to outlaw the point after touchdown. He termed himself the "Kingfish" after a blackface character on the "Amos 'n' Andy" radio

Huey Long (left) assails the New Deal in 1935 after being branded "political enemy number one" by General Hugh Johnson of the NRA. Long's assassination and the shooting of his killer, Dr Carl A. Weiss, are depicted in John McCrady's painting (right).

UPI

program. He outraged and shocked, but he also brought free schoolbooks, roads, bridges, and hope to the ignorant and frustrated lives of poor southern whites.

When his enemies succeeeded in stalling his programs in 1931, the Kingfish turned a primary contest for the US Senate into a popular referendum on the issues by entering his own name. Long won the primary, his programs were adopted, and he went on to the Senate.

There was never any question of Senator Long giving up his iron-fisted control of Louisiana. He appointed a henchman with the appropriate name of O.K. Allen to be governor, but not before the lieutenant governor moved into the vacant office and Long had him arrested as an impostor.

Even in Washington the Kingfish seemed determined to break every rule possible. He upset the august dignity of the Senate so much that Kenneth McKellar of Tennessee said, ''I don't think Huey Long could get the Lord's prayer endorsed in this body.'' It hardly mattered because Long soon had more interest in the White House than the Senate anyway. He turned his scathing tongue to the likes of New Dealers Henry Wallace, Harold Ickes, and General Hugh Johnson, whom he referred to respectively as ''King Corn,'' the ''Chicago Chinch Bug,'' and ''Sitting Bull.'' General Johnson blustered that Long was ''political enemy number one,'' while

Harold Ickes disdainfully remarked that ''the emperor of Louisiana has halitosis of the intellect.''

The senator had progressed from reformer and political evangelist to a demagogue with the sinister overtones of a dictator. There could be no doubt about the brilliance that lurked behind the inelegant exterior, but there were real fears about the ruthless ambitions that drove him toward power like a crazed bear to honey. Ickes's ''emperor'' ruled Louisiana like an oriental potentate. He once had the legislature pass forty-four bills in two hours, a move that even caused comment in London where *The Times* worried aloud that ''honest government and democratic institutions have disappeared from Louisiana . . . the enactments smack more of Nazi Germany than Democratic America.'' At home, observers like Norton McGiffin were even more pointed: ''The Louisiana kingfish is the embryonic Hitler who undoubtedly plans a *putsch* to carry him into the White House.''

Ridicule turned to real concern as Long continued to garner support with promises and ideas that America's poor had hardly dared to dream about. His ''Share-Our-Wealth'' plan promised to provide a home, auto, and radio for every deserving family by limiting the size of personal fortunes to $5 million. It seemed to McGiffin that ''Huey Long is the poor man's choice for president [in 1936] . . . he would only have to draw 5 million votes from Mr Roosevelt to elect a Republican.''

Huey Long was well aware that his enemies were legion. He had for years lived in fear of assassination and surrounded himself with a shotgun brigade of personal attendants. But on the night of Sunday, September 8, 1935, as the forty-two year old Long was hurrying along a passage in the new capitol building in Baton Rouge, Dr Carl A. Weiss brushed past the bodyguards and fired a single shot into the senator's stomach. Weiss was instantly floored by a resounding volley from Long's men that riddled him with sixty-one bullets.

It took Huey Pierce Long two days to die, and when he did it was as if Robin Hood himself had been murdered. The Louisiana legislature gave him a state funeral, had his body interred in the capitol grounds, and erected a monument over his grave. They placed a bronze statue of him in the National Statuary Hall in Washington and made his birthday a state holiday. Hospitals and bridges were named after him. His house was made a memorial. Huey Long was gone, but it would be impossible to forget him.

month, provided that the money be spent within thirty days. In many places, including Minneapolis and the Central Valley of California, workers engaged in strikes and riots, often encouraged by Communists and others of the Left but basically stimulated by the general dissatisfaction with the economic situation. The unusually intense class warfare of 1934 persuaded Democratic Senator Robert Wagner of New York that the national government must make much greater efforts to help workers develop strong, independent unions.

Pressures for change mounted inside as well as outside the Roosevelt administration. Some of it came from disciples of Justice Louis Brandeis, who disliked the centralization of power promoted by the National Industrial Recovery Act and advocated action by the national government to decentralize power and restore competition. Other government officials, including Marriner Eccles of the Federal Reserve Board, believed that Washington should use its taxing and spending powers—its fiscal policy—more boldly to promote recovery and should enlarge its power over the actual supply of money—its monetary policy—into an instrument of control over the business cycle. Social reformers, headed by Frances Perkins, the secretary of labor, developed plans for old-age pensions and unemployment insurance, while planners and reformers in the department of agriculture, including Rexford Tugwell, M. L.

Wilson, and Jerome Frank, sought ways to serve more than the interests of commercial farmers.

In the fall of 1934, the voters demonstrated that they preferred advocates of government action and rejected the retreat to past practices. The Democrats enjoyed an impressive victory that filled the House with 322 Democrats and only 122 Republicans; sixty-nine Democrats and twenty-seven Republicans went to the Senate. Before 1934, the party in the White House had usually lost ground in the congressional elections held between contests for the presidency. The results this time encouraged advocates of change, like Senator Wagner and Harry Hopkins, the head of the relief programs, to believe that their ambitions for reform would be fulfilled. However, in 1935 and early 1936 the Supreme Court presented a formidable obstacle, demonstrating a very negative attitude toward govern-

Depression drew class lines with more feeling and clarity than ever before in America. The wealthy saw themselves threatened as the unions expanded and as many Americans toyed with socialism and communism. The ostentatiously rich red plush of Reginald Marsh's Monday Night at the Metropolitan *(right) is in sharp contrast to the spareness and severity of purpose of the left-wing journal,* New Masses *(below).*

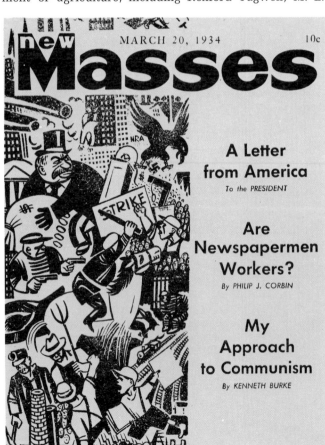

Both pictures: With appreciation to The British Museum Newspaper Section/John Freeman

ment action in social and economic affairs. Three members of the Court, Louis Brandeis, Harlan Fiske Stone, and Benjamin Cardozo, did argue that judges should use their power very cautiously and be quite tolerant of government attacks upon social and economic problems. A larger group, however, composed of Willis Van Devanter, James C. McReynolds, George Sutherland, and Pierce Butler, were inclined to use their power boldly in the area of government-business relations, believing in the changeless character of the Constitution and the scientific, objective nature of judicial review. Public opinion, in their view, was irrelevant and the Court was responsible for saving society from its own irrational tendencies. The other members of the Court, Charles Evans Hughes, the Chief Justice, and Owen J. Roberts, tended to vote with the conservative bloc (Van Devanter and his allies).

All of the justices had been appointed by Roosevelt's

Justice Harlan Stone (right) argued "self-restraint" for the Supreme Court, but a majority of his colleagues struck out boldly at the New Deal in the Schecter *and* Butler *cases. The Schecter brothers (below) were jubilant after the NRA was ruled unconstitutional.*

predecessors, and now they attacked two of his most important programs. In the *Schecter* case of May 27, 1935, the Court declared that the National Industrial Recovery Act was an unconstitutional delegation of power and also an unconstitutional attempt to regulate intrastate business. In the *Butler* case of January 6, 1936, the majority ruled that the Agricultural Adjustment Act violated the Constitution by attempting to regulate production and by using taxes as a penalty in an effort to control activities that were otherwise beyond the reach of Congress. These decisions amounted to an unusually vigorous exercise of judicial power and placed severe restrictions on the ability of the national government to solve economic problems. Harlan Stone charged that the majority of the justices had come to think of the Court as the "only agency of government that must be assumed to have capacity to govern."

Help for the Lower Paid

The New Deal was being challenged from many directions. In this difficult situation, Roosevelt demonstrated a willingness to compromise as well as to push for further action. He endorsed new ideas, lending them the prestige of the presidency, and then battled for them in Congress. The direction taken was especially toward action on behalf of lower-income groups, even though it risked further troubles with business interests and the Supreme Court. It seemed to FDR that it was not only his future, but the future of the Republic that was at stake.

The early emphasis upon government-business cooperation of 1933–34 was put aside. There was no attempt to revive the National Recovery Administration after the Court killed it, but substitutes for the NRA were supplied for specific industries, including coal mining and trucking. New tax and regulatory legislation concerned with the concentration of wealth, Wall Street, and the public utility holding companies attacked the size and power of business and banking institutions. However, these laws were not forceful enough to be successful.

More was achieved in the area of welfare activities than in the direct attacks upon big business. A new relief agency, still headed by Hopkins, replaced the old Civil Works Administration. The Works Progress Administration was established in the spring of 1935 and given $1.4 billion to begin its operations. An enlargement of national relief efforts, the WPA emphasized work relief, seeking to give jobs to as many people as possible and to employ them in tasks that they were equipped by training and experience to handle. Although raking leaves and leaning on shovels became symbols of WPA for its critics, the agency employed many people constructing public buildings and developing transportation and recreational

facilities; these were contributions of value. Unfortunately, the agency's appropriation allowed it to give employment to only a minority of the unemployed.

Another feature of the "welfare state" that was taking shape was the system of social security. Frances Perkins, a former social worker, played a leading role in the development of the new legislation. The Social Security Act set up a national plan of old-age insurance which covered most workers, except those in farming, government, and education. Every person over sixty-five would receive a retirement pension financed equally out of own earnings and contributions by employers. The federal government also promised to help the states care for those already retired and not qualified for coverage. And finally, the act established state unemployment insurance schemes, again paid for by a tax on both employer and employed. The reformers assumed that society must supply programs to protect old people and wage earners against some of the major hazards of life in an urban industrial society. The advance of the welfare state represented more than a response to the depression. The depression had enlarged support for long-standing social theories and programs, persuading millions of people that society had defects that must be remedied by relief and social security plans. These new programs had serious limitations; they excluded many workers and taxed others. Yet the legislation constituted a significant step forward.

The New Dealers also modified the New Deal for agriculture in 1935 and 1936. In April 1935, Roosevelt

The growth of the welfare state seemed to many to presage the loss of individuality. Below: A vision of social security reducing the citizen to a number.

established a new independent agency, the Resettlement Administration, to grapple with the problems of the rural poor, problems such as poor land, small land holdings, insecure tenure arrangements, and migration from farm to farm. The officials of the new agency developed a battery of programs, hoping to hit the problems from several directions. It was assumed that the plight of the rural poor had to be attacked directly; small farmers, farmers on poor land, sharecroppers, migratory workers, and other rural people living below the poverty line should not be forced to wait for benefits to trickle down to them from programs designed to deal directly with the problems of other groups.

Other new rural programs took shape in 1935 as well. The Rural Electrification Administration provided power to farms and homes that private power companies could not or would not previously supply. The study of the land and the soil was raised to the status of a science by the Soil Conservation Act. The changes in the agricultural sector added up to an elaborate set of programs designed to continue the efforts of the early New Deal to make farming a profitable business. At the same time and in the same programs, the national government was trying to reform and improve rural life.

Government Aid for the Unions

During this time also, the federal government embarked upon a major and highly significant effort to promote the development and growth of labor unions. The Wagner or National Labor Relations Act was passed in 1935. Senator Wagner had been battling for this legislation for some time, although FDR did not endorse it until it reached an advanced stage in Congress. Wagner believed that strong labor unions could give the workers the purchasing power needed for recovery and prosperity and strengthen the working classes politically. Government help was needed for the labor movement to overcome strong opposition from powerful business interests.

When Congress passed Wagner's proposal by wide margins in both House and Senate, the action provided an especially significant demonstration of the importance of the 1934 elections. They had not silenced opponents of change in such important areas as labor-management relations, but they had given great strength to its advocates.

A barefoot tenant farmer stares at erosion-wasted land. The Resettlement Administration assisted poor farmers with loans to help them purchase their land and with advice about matters like soil conservation and land reclamation.

49

According to the Wagner Act, workers had the right to bargain collectively in unions of their own choosing, and business leaders must no longer employ the weapons they had used in the past to prevent workers from enjoying that right. A new agency, the National Labor Relations Board, was empowered to enforce the act. The legislation was a sharp break with the past. Now, government became more active in labor-management relations and more friendly to unions.

While frequently bold in 1935–36, Congress and the administration continued to pursue a comparatively cautious fiscal policy. Despite greatly increased pressures, federal spending rose only from $6.5 billion in the 1935 fiscal year (ending June 30, 1935) to $8.5 billion the following year, and the deficit in the federal budget (the gap between income and expenditures) increased only from $2.6 billion to $3.5 billion. Roosevelt's own attitudes exerted a restraining influence here. He did not endorse the argument that the quest for recovery alone justified government spending, and he insisted that a spending proposal be justified in other ways, such as the construction of a valuable dam or building would be. And he continued to stress that the budget would be balanced as soon as possible. While he could now brush aside arguments about damage to business confidence when considering proposals that seemed very valuable to him, like social security, such arguments exerted a strong influence upon him when deciding levels of spending. He did not want to frighten and discourage businessmen with large-scale expenditures and deficits.

In 1935–36, shifts in emphasis had taken place. The federal government expanded a great deal in this period and it became more responsive to the needs of lower-income groups and more critical of business groups. The government remained committed to capitalism, but it now tried harder than it had earlier to reduce the size of business organizations, although such attempts were a small part of the New Deal. Much greater efforts were aimed at the reduction of business power but chiefly by strengthening government and labor, not by breaking up large business organizations. The reproportioning of power, it was assumed, would lead to a more equitable distribution of wealth and income and to prosperity.

Roosevelt's 1936 Election Triumph

Roosevelt and the New Deal moved on to a spectacular victory at the polls in November 1936. While largely the result of the depression and the New Deal, the victory owed something to Roosevelt's reelection strategy. Party affiliations were played down in the desire for a large majority. Roosevelt recognized that his party had been weak for many years and had been able to win presiden-

Above: The Review of Reviews *in June of 1935 saw Roosevelt as the Good Samaritan. The president's fiscal policy was to revive the economy with federal funds, but not at the expense of private incentive.*

tial elections only when the Republicans fell apart, as they did in 1912, or staggered under the blows of a great national calamity, such as in 1932. He had no desire to rely on party loyalties for there were not enough people who looked upon themselves as Democrats of long standing. FDR seldom referred to the Democratic party and went out of his way to encourage Republicans and independents to vote for him and his allies. The voters were also reminded of the dismal conditions of 1932, contrasting them with the improvements made since. He made a strong appeal to class feelings, picturing the leaders of big business as his enemies and portraying himself as the friend and champion of the many millions of Americans in the lower-income groups.

A personal victory was Roosevelt's most obvious goal, but he also had a significant change in view. He hoped to establish a new political party. He would not change the name; it would continue to be called the Democratic party. It would not be a neat, cohesive party united around a point of view. It would not be a liberal party

Library of Congress

Above: A family of poor blacks stand outside their ramshackle house for a photograph. The New Deal aided black workers, often especially hard hit by the depression, and won their votes.

set apart at every point from conservative and radical parties. It would, however, be a new party, much larger than the old Democratic party, much stronger in the North and West than the old one was, less dependent upon the South, and more attractive to lower-income Americans.

Roosevelt achieved just the kind of victory that he desired. It was a landslide in which 28 million Americans voted for him while only 17 million voted Republican. He gained more than 60 per cent of the popular vote and 523 of the 531 electoral votes. At the same time, the Democratic party increased its margins of control in Congress, moving from 69 to 75 senators out of 96 and from 322 to 333 representatives out of 435.

Roosevelt, aided by the depression and the New Deal, had put together a new political coalition, at least for this election. The largest element was the urban working classes. They gave Roosevelt even more votes than they had in 1932, thereby expressing their enthusiasm for the benefits that they had received from the federal government since that year. Many of these people were first or second-generation Americans who believed in and benefited from FDR's social and economic programs. These groups of "new stock" backgrounds also appreciated the new appointment policies which rejected racist

attitudes and assumed that others than "White Anglo-Saxon Protestants" (WASPs) were also capable of making valuable contributions to America.

A major change had taken place in the political behavior of the largely urban black voters. In the past, they had voted for Republican presidential candidates. This had been true even in 1932. The change had occurred despite the fact that the New Deal included no civil rights programs, such as antilynching legislation, and was tarnished by discrimination and segregation in many places. The first to be unemployed, however, urban blacks received substantial help from the New Deal. Other blacks also voted for Roosevelt and for other reasons as well, including the appointment policies that increased very significantly the number of blacks in federal positions.

Organized labor, another important element in the coalition, also gave Roosevelt much more support than in 1932. Some labor leaders moved to him from the Republican party; others moved from the Socialist party.

Labor liked both his help to workers and his help to unions, and the leaders worked successfully to persuade workers to go to the polls. The unions made important financial contributions to the Democratic campaign, compensating for the sharp decline in support from business.

The largest gains had been made in the cities, but the Democratic coalition also contained more farmers than ever before. Gains came in the Far West and the Middle West in spite of the strength of Republican traditions in those regions. There was disgust with the Republicans for their response to the farm depression, which had begun before 1929, and gratitude for New Deal farm programs.

Many people had been added to the Democratic party, but the old props, the city machines and the South, remained in place. They had not been knocked over by the influx of new people. The bosses liked the increase in patronage that the New Deal produced. Organizations that cooperated with the Roosevelt administration, like the Pendergast machine in Kansas City, won from the New Deal an opportunity to increase their strength. Members of such organizations administered important programs, like the WPA, on state and local levels, and found new ways to increase support. New Deal beneficiaries expressed their gratitude by voting for the machine's candidates, as in the past they had said thanks for food baskets, picnics, and other benefits that the machine supplied.

Southerners had traditionally voted Democratic, and Roosevelt held onto their support by a margin of more than three to one. Most southerners liked the New Deal. Their representatives had contributed significantly to the development of it. Some southern Democrats disliked it, but they were restrained by their attachment to their party and by Roosevelt's great popularity in the South.

One of the few Democrats who defected in 1936 was the party's presidential candidate of 1928, Al Smith. The desertion of the Democrats by Smith, who had been FDR's early political mentor, and a few others who disliked the New Deal, fell far short of the troubles of the Republican party.

The Fate of the Other Parties

Embarrassed by the depression and wracked by internal conflict, the Republican party had lost its status as the nation's majority party, a position it had enjoyed from the depression of the 1890s to the Great Depression of the 1930s. Internal conflict revolved around the question of the party's relations with the New Deal. Should Republicans firmly oppose the changes that were taking place, or should they go along with them? The party selected a moderately progressive candidate for the

presidency, Governor Alf Landon of Kansas, a man who found much to admire in the New Deal and had cooperated frequently with the Roosevelt administration. Yet he did give the voters a choice in 1936. He promised to administer the federal government more efficiently and to cut costs, and he made other commitments that suggested that the federal government would not be quite so large and quite so expensive if he were president.

Only slightly more than a third of the voters selected Landon, but the election demonstrated quite dramatically that the depression had not destroyed the influence of traditions. Most of those who voted for Landon were old-stock, Protestant Americans living in the rural areas, towns, and suburbs. Few of them were poor. Some Republican voters were returning to their traditional party while others were expressing hostility toward the ways in which the country was being changed. To many of his supporters, Landon symbolized an older, simpler, and better America.

But the Republican party seemed to be the party of big business, and most voters did not have great enthusiasm for that part of American life in 1936. The support that the Grand Old Party received from the Liberty League helped many voters conclude that the party was controlled by big business and unsympathetic to the people who had suffered from the depression. The league had become increasingly active in response to the political developments of 1935–36. After toying with the idea of sponsoring a third party, it had endorsed Landon and spent millions of dollars in efforts to have him elected. These contributions embarrassed the Republican candidate, who did not always agree with the Liberty Leaguers, and provided Democrats with a potent argument to use against him and his party. The election had a devastating impact upon the league. It had tried so hard and had failed so dismally. The outcome demoralized the group, and it soon ceased to participate in American politics.

Roosevelt frustrated the Left as well as the Right. Thomas, running for a third time for the presidency as the Socialist candidate, received only 200,000 votes. Roosevelt's New Deal had undermined the Socialists and half of the party's members deserted soon after the election. Former members, like Sidney Hillman and David Dubinsky, two prominent labor leaders, had shifted their allegiance by 1936, convinced that the Socialist party had no chance of success in the United States. They felt the New Deal was making improvements even though it was not moving the nation from capitalism to socialism. More important, Roosevelt had gained the support of the working people that the Socialists had been counting upon for success. Had Roosevelt and the New Deal not been present and had Thomas faced only much more conservative opponents, the Socialist movement might have obtained the support of the American workers that it needed for success in the 1930s.

The Liberty party also suffered defeat in 1936. The movement it represented had been weakened by the assassination of Huey Long late in 1935, but Coughlin and others had attempted to unite their followers with Long's and Townsend's into a broad national movement. They had hoped to attract 9 million voters in 1936. Rather confused intellectually, the new party denounced the New Deal as both "bent on communistic revolution" and dominated by "international bankers." The people responded by giving the group fewer than 1 million votes. Coughlin retired from politics for a time, humiliated by his failure to deliver on his promise to drive "a Communist from a chair once occupied by Washington."

American radicals, both the variety represented by Coughlin and the brand for which Thomas spoke, had again failed to gain a significant amount of support from lower-income Americans. Nearly 40 per cent of the adults were not motivated to go to the polls in 1936. The Left actually had less success than Roosevelt did in persuading people to vote. Roosevelt, with his program and his personality, had successfully exploited the opportunities for party realignment that existed in the 1930s. Largely because of his attractiveness, voter turnout was higher than it had been for many years. A combination of traditional attachment to the Democratic party and interest in non-revolutionary change had altered the relations between the two major parties. In sharp contrast with the situation that had prevailed for so many years before, the largest bloc of voters now thought of the Democratic party as their party.

Fighting the "Nine Old Men"

Having triumphed over challenges from the Left and the Right, Roosevelt turned on the Supreme Court, which seemed to threaten the New Deal. FDR was influenced by his fear that the justices would invalidate major features of the new programs. In 1936, the Court overturned an effort by the federal government to regulate labor-management relations, and then a state law establishing a minimum wage for women. These decisions suggested to Roosevelt that the Social Security program and the Wagner Act would be in jeopardy as soon as they moved up to the high court.

After considering the problem for many months, the president rejected a proposed constitutional amendment as the solution. He concluded that while an amendment curbing the power of the Court could be devised, too many states might reject the amendment. Even if the necessary number of states could be persuaded to accept the change, the New Deal would lie in a shambles before the long amendment process had reached its conclusion.

Rather than propose a change in the Constitution, Roosevelt decided to rely upon well-established powers to

The "Nine Old Men" of the Supreme Court were lampooned by the New Masses. *FDR was not alone in thinking that the Court threatened the existence of the New Deal in 1937.*

53

*A cartoon of the president's shatteringly
unsuccessful attempt to pack the Supreme
Court with his own men. Roosevelt was severely
chastised for daring to tamper with the Court.*

alter the behavior of the Court. He called upon Congress to pass a law authorizing him (and his successors) to add a justice for every member of the Court who was more than seventy years old and yet chose not to retire. The composition of the Court, not the institution itself, FDR believed, was the source of the problem. New and younger members would be more sensitive to social and economic problems.

Fresh from his spectacular victory and accustomed to cooperation from Congress, the president expected that Congress would accept his proposal. Most congressmen, however, disappointed him. There was a tradition of distrust of the Court as an undemocratic institution because it was composed of men who had been appointed to office and served as long as they chose to do so. But, now, another old attitude surfaced. The Court was held in reverence as the defender of the Constitution and the protector of the rights of individuals and minorities. To many people it looked as if Roosevelt really did mean to become a dictator. Congressmen who had been reluctant to express their criticisms of the president earlier

now felt free to do so, and others who had been sincere supporters now moved into the opposition on this issue. Too weak to accomplish much, the Republicans discovered that they did not need to engage in open battle on this issue. Democrats were available for combat on the side of the opposition. After a five-month struggle, the contest came to an end in July 1937 with Roosevelt's surrender.

Roosevelt did not surrender, however, until after the Court had begun to behave in new ways. That change, in fact, contributed significantly to his defeat by making the reform seem unnecessary, and the change also enabled him to claim that he had won the war. Overturning old doctrines and old decisions, the Court now upheld a state law that established a minimum wage for women, and, even more significant from FDR's point of view, upheld two major elements in the New Deal, the Wagner Act and Social Security.

The Court changed its behavior even though it was still composed of the same men who had produced so many problems for and threats to the New Deal. Although he had been in office for more than four years, Roosevelt had not yet had a chance to appoint anyone to this very important institution.

The change resulted from shifts by two members of the Court, Hughes and Roberts. They deserted the conservatives and voted with the liberals in the spring of 1937. Like Roosevelt, they now feared that if major elements of the obviously popular New Deal were destroyed, millions of people might erupt in protest, demand that the Court's powers be curbed or even destroyed, and move beyond that to strong attacks on other major parts of American life. The people had spoken clearly in November 1936. Since then, intense conflict between labor and management over the organization of workers suggested that not everyone would passively accept the destruction by nine old men of essential elements of the New Deal.

Roosevelt had created troubles for himself with the Congress, as would become more obvious in the next two years, but he had helped to secure the programs that had already been established when relations between the White House and Capitol Hill had been more harmonious. The Court had been only one of the serious challenges that he had faced from 1935 to 1937; radicals, conservatives, and Republicans outside the Court had also threatened him. If they had placed limits on his accomplishments, they had not defeated him, and they had stimulated him to new achievements. Roosevelt and the Congress had made important changes in the New Deal. The president and his party had enjoyed spectacular victories at the polls that realigned the two major parties and seriously damaged both the right and the left wings of the political spectrum. The Supreme Court had changed its attitude toward the New Deal. It was a period of dramatic innovations. And these innovations seemed capable of surviving beyond the summer of 1937.

Chapter 3

SOCIETY DURING THE DEPRESSION

The effects of the Great Depression touched the lives of every American. Although the wealthy continued to live in a manner that must have seemed obscene to many at the time, the less fortunate saw the disappearance of their savings, an end to work, and an end to immediate hopes for a better standard of living. The depression years, in this respect, were the "standstill years." While many were forced to live on the breadline, those who were lucky enough to hold a steady job just tightened their belts and waited for better times. Their days were enlivened by numerous forms of entertainment. And sporting heroes raised the pulse of millions who, for a while at least, could forget the harsh realities of everyday life.

Coping with Hard Times

The Great Depression is remembered to us in grim or romantic images. We picture crowds of people standing in front of closed factory gates, or moving like their pioneer ancestors across the plains, or listening to orators in Union Square, or holding automobile plants against company armies. Survivors are still proud of the endurance they shared with others of their generation. Some who voted for Roosevelt and belonged to the democratic impulse of the time have now turned their experiences into a conservative rhetoric as they murmur about a young generation that knows nothing of hardship and its virtues. The poignant images of the period are valid to a degree, but the Great Depression is interesting also in the smaller or indirect effects that came of it, the shapes that society took on under its influence.

Statistics alone fail to convey to later generations the desperation of the 1930s. Pictures of the poor, such as those of farm workers by Dorothea Lange or Walker Evans, impart something of what poverty did to people. Fiction also achieves this end: Sherwood Anderson's characterization in *Puzzled America* of a man thrown out of work in a southern industrial town ("It was an everyday, common enough story"); James T. Farrell's portrayal of young Studs Lonigan searching for a job in Chicago; John Steinbeck's chronicle of the vicissitudes of a migrant family in *The Grapes of Wrath* ("failure hangs over [California] like a great sorrow"); James Agee's stark evocation of the southern sharecroppers in *Let Us Now Praise Famous Men* ("It is simple and terrible work"); Ruth McKenney's accounts of the Akron rubber workers and the CIO sitdown strikes in *Industrial Valley;* Erskine Caldwell's short stories; Edmund Wilson's essays; Muriel Rukeyser's poetry; Woody Guthrie's songs. "The fog of despair hung over the land," Arthur Schlesinger, Jr, wrote at the beginning of *The Crisis of the Old Order;* the writers of the decade caught that despair in a way that tables, charts, and graphs do not.

Still another angle of vision is provided in the popular social history of the thirties, Frederick Lewis Allen's *Since Yesterday.* In numerous small images Allen charted the decade: walking from place to place looking for jobs; borrowing from relatives; accepting relief payments. An observant man might notice the vacant stores, the lethargic factories, the absence of construction noise, and certainly the panhandlers. Traveling by railroad, he might see that trains were shorter and Pullman cars fewer; he could not fail to spot the ramshackle "Hoovervilles" on the outskirts of towns, the drifters of all ages and both sexes, homeless people sleeping in doorways or in fields alongside train tracks or highways.

Then as now, hard times struck first the unskilled, those least likely to possess resources to tide them over. Particular geographical areas were hardest hit: the southern Appalachians with their depleted resources; the Great Plains made barren by wind erosion and drought; the old southern cotton belt, suffering from too much population pressure on too few resources. Essential skilled workers, both farm and factory, or those in the few powerful unions, usually rode out the decade relatively unscathed; their wages declined less swiftly than prices. Clerks, typists, and many white collar workers fared less well as business slowed. Professionals like lawyers and doctors suffered a steep income decline, reflecting the lagging earnings of their clients. Schoolteaching, especially in college, was usually a stable, much-prized job though sometimes beset by lowered wages. Government work became most desirable of all; Washington, DC, possessed the healthiest economy of any city in the nation.

For small businessmen lucky enough to survive until New Deal "alphabet agencies" ended deflation, the Roosevelt era restored a measure of stability. Though banks hoarded money, making long-term expansion almost impossible, grocers, druggists, and fuel dealers, for example, could rely upon a small but stable income, low taxes, and slowly appreciating assets. After 1933, storekeepers rarely worried about paying the rent or sending the children to college. In fact, many merchants took advantage of abysmally low prices to invest in land or the stock market. As the years passed, however, more and more middle-class entrepreneurs criticized New Deal "experiments." They carped that government controls needlessly complicated business affairs; they fretted that high taxes might take away high profits, if prosperity ever returned. A few probably realized that depression had badly battered middle-class self-confidence and America's well-deserved reputation for innovation. Times were not good for the small, independent businessman, and he was losing his central role in the American economy, but then times were not all bad either.

Except for the worst months at the end of 1932 and the beginning of 1933, depression had not much affected the very rich, that top 5 per cent of the population who owned three-fourths of the nation's wealth. The stock market crash had wiped out unwise plungers, not those whose investments were carefully diversified. Although dividends and rents declined during those long, weary years, prices also went down. Ice cubes still tinkled against cut glass at cocktail parties, though now such affairs moved back into expensive apartments away from dimly-lit speak-easies. Well-dressed women copied Parisian styles,

Some Americans could afford to continue to live as they had before the depression. McCall's magazine (top) and Vogue *(below) kept the fashion-conscious aware of the latest styles from "casual country" to "tropic" wear.*

BROOKE HANLON   FRANCES NOYES HART

VINCENT SHEEAN   EVELYN GILL KLAHR

McCall's/Transworld Feature Syndicate, NY

Best in the Show: Fabrics for casual country clothes . . . supple in weave, beautiful in color . . . are merely a part of the complete range of woolens made by the famous Hockanum Mills for Fall 1936. From the most formal coatings to the sheerest of sheer fabrics for dresses, they all have the tailoring quality that only genuinely fine materials can achieve. Coats, suits, and dresses made of these fabrics are now being featured by the best shops and department stores throughout the country.

Hockanum Mills, Rockville, Conn. Founded 1809; Division of M. T. Stevens & Sons Company, North Andover, Mass. J. P. Stevens & Co., Inc., Selling Agents, 261 Fifth Avenue, New York.

HOCKANUM Woolens

New care-free clothes

Your southern clothes of the new Forstmann Fabrics will have a casual, care-free loveliness that comes from the very practical idea behind their creation: the great need for fabrics that are cooler and more adapted to warm weather wear. They keep fresh and trim in tropic heat and ocean dampness. And their colors! They are the most flattering made, and resist sun and perspiration to a degree never before achieved. You can get them made up in costumes or in the yard at all better shops . . . or write Forstmann Woolen Co., Passaic, N. J. Sales Office: Empire State Bldg., N. Y. C.

Forstmann Woolens

wearing long scarves, low hemlines, and close-fitting hats. The rich collected objets d'art during the 1930s. Porcelain, antique silver, paintings, French furniture, and jewelry flooded into the United States as the wealthy bought treasures from Europe's harder-pressed upper classes. Winter vacationing in Florida and the Caribbean became popular, with Miami and Havana the new watering holes for the very fashionable. More and more islands built resort hotels and legalized casino gambling; even American administrators in Puerto Rico and the Virgin Islands gave in to the universal effort to lure rich tourists from New York and Chicago. On the mainland, conspicuous consumption revived, though not the open lavishness of the twenties. General Motors reported large declines in sales of Chevrolets, but continued demand for Cadillacs. The Canadian fur business experienced a boom when *Vogue* magazine decreed mink for the winter of 1935. Manhattan matrons talked once again of "the servant problem." Depression neither narrowed the gap between rich and poor nor permanently reduced the living standards of America's rich.

Though their sybaritic pleasures continued almost uninterruptedly, the very rich realized that they no longer had such control over America's destiny. Perhaps this loss of power explained their irrational hatred of Franklin D. Roosevelt, "that man in the White House," who had, many thought, "betrayed his class." Tales of Roosevelt's insanity, of strange laughter in the night, found a ready credence among usually skeptical wealthy businessmen; lurid jokes slurred both president and First Lady. Yet, in propping up the capitalist system, the New Deal had secured the wealthy in their property. Overlooking this irony, many American millionaires piously worried about a decline in self-reliance among the working classes or ritually complained about high taxes—though in 1936 the tax on a $1 million income increased only $1,800, about two-tenths of 1 per cent. Their anger was not over economic loss, but a realization that the failures of business society during the Hoover years had permanently stripped them of independent power. Only a few of the enormously wealthy—men like John D. Rockefeller, Jr, for example, who replaced nine square blocks of Manhattan slums with skyscrapers without borrowing from any bank—could exercise that unbridled power which the wealthy, as a class, had lost. Big government now regulated their self-enrichment and even competed with them for control of America's future. No wonder they hated the symbol of this new order: Roosevelt had given them back riches but had taken away both power and public prestige.

Charitable agencies did much to alleviate distress and hardship among those who were most severely hit by the depression. Home Relief Station *was painted by Louis Ribak in 1935–36.*

Making Ends Meet

For the average American, loss of employment, or the threat of it, had a startling impact on his social customs. Even the fabric of family sagged under economic adversity, which could undermine parental authority and force children out of the home. Sometimes the very identification of home and family ended as banks foreclosed mortgages. Although the birth rate had fallen gradually since the 1890s, American parents became so discouraged that between 1935 and 1940 the number of new babies dropped below zero growth rate. Young couples postponed children until times improved, and for the same reason the number of marriages decreased by nearly one-fourth. Only because deaths dropped to eleven per thousand—boosting life expectancy to 63 years—did the population increase as much as 7 per cent in the course of the decade. For somewhat obscure reasons the number of divorces dropped sharply; certainly lawyers and settlement costs were beyond the reach of most people.

The greatest distortions in American family life were less tangible. Across the country, indigent relatives moved in with more fortunate aunts or brothers or cousins. Generations crowded in on each other, grandmothers and mothers arguing over how to raise children or run the household. Youngsters were suddenly confronted with orders from many adults, not just two. Rising unemployment forced women back into the home, often breaking short the chance for a more independent life hinted at during the 1920s. Most available jobs for men went to unskilled laborers at low wages; railroads, for example, paid only $10 a week for work on road gangs. As a result, fathers often sat at home, losing their traditional authority over the family while their sons worked.

During the depths of the depression many Americans discovered new ways to earn a living. In the 1920s people had avoided jury duty; now they crowded into the criminal courts building, eager to receive the $4 for each day they served. An army of new salesmen went from door to door peddling everything imaginable; in cities they spread out their wares along the streets. Arguments went on over whether permanent investment in a shoe shine kit was better than hawking apples or newspapers. Sunday papers sold from door to door in apartment houses proved a lucrative endeavor, and more and more newsboys walked the side streets with reasonable success. The vegetable or fruit pushcart reappeared.

For America at large this portrait delivered by a traveler to a congressional committee in 1932 is not wide of the mark:

In the State of Washington I was told that the forest fires raging in that region all summer and fall

Courtesy Museum of Fine Arts, Boston. Hayden Collection

Many of the unemployed resorted to selling goods or services. Above: George Grosz's Shoeshine *portrays one of the depression's most poignant symbols. Right: This 1932 photograph shows an apple vendor awaiting business beside a Republican campaign headquarters in Pennsylvania.*

were caused by unemployed timber workers and bankrupt farmers in an endeavor to earn a few honest dollars as fire fighters. The last thing I saw on the night I left Seattle was numbers of women searching for scraps of food in the refuse piles of the principal market of that city. A number of Montana citizens told me of thousands of bushels of wheat left in the fields uncut on account of its low price that hardly paid for the harvesting. In Oregon I saw thousands of bushels of apples rotting in the orchards.

While I was in Oregon the Portland *Oregonian* bemoaned the fact that thousands of ewes were killed by the sheep raisers because they did not bring enough in the market to pay the freight on them. And while Oregon sheep raisers fed mutton to the buzzards, I saw men picking for meat scraps in the garbage cans in . . . New York and Chicago.

Thousands took whatever work was available in order to make enough money merely to stay alive. Below: Farm workers' dilapidated homes. Inset: Cotton workers walking a Colorado road in 1936 follow the crop.

The roads of the West and Southwest teem with hungry hitchhikers. The camp fires of the homeless are seen along every railroad track. I saw men, women, and children walking over the hard roads. Most of them were tenant farmers who had lost their all in the late slump in wheat and cotton.

As a result of this appalling overproduction on the one side and the staggering underconsumption on the other side, 70 per cent of the farmers of Oklahoma were unable to pay the interests on their mortgages. Last week one of the largest and oldest mortgage companies in that State went into the hands of the receiver. In that and other States we have now the interesting spectacle of farmers losing their farms by foreclosure and mortgage companies losing their recouped holdings by tax sales.

The farmers are being pauperized by the poverty of industrial populations and the industrial populations are being pauperized by the poverty of the farmers. Neither has the money to buy the products of the other; hence we have overproduction and underconsumption at the same time and in the same country.

Many tried to escape family tensions and an unpromising future. For the first time since the frontier had disappeared in the late nineteenth century, Americans once again bustled about in large numbers. Attachment to place evaporated for millions. By 1940 about 60 per cent of the people lived in urban areas, and rural population

An Arkansas blacksmith and his family pause to change a tire in Oklahoma in 1938. Families like this suffered the dislocation and degradation that went with the search for employment.

had declined by more than a fifth in the course of the decade. Drought and low commodity prices forced many midwesterners toward California or into middle-sized towns. Whole families, unable to find work or to continue the rent or payments on the home, piled into the old car and took to the highway only to be driven—bewildered bits of humanity—from town to town by a strange force called a "depression." Migratory workers usually moved with the seasons, but some simply rushed into regions where, rumor had it, jobs existed. Perhaps as many as 5 million people became vagrants, perpetually unemployed, perpetually hounded out of towns. These vagrants "rode the rails" or gathered together in camps remote from state troopers. About 900,000 tramps were children, not yet eighteen years old. Union Pacific Railroad reported in 1933 that freight cars had killed hundreds of these inexperienced boys and girls. For nearly a sixth of the population, depression meant permanent emigration, always leaving some place, never really going anywhere.

The New Deal grappled with the consequences of this mass rootlessness but never repaired the harsh psychological damage inflicted upon the victims of depression. Between 1933 and 1941 the Civilian Conservation Corps (CCC) employed 2.5 million young men in reforestation and flood control projects. Meager and belated help came for migratory farm workers. By 1939 the New Deal had set up thirty regional camps, which accommodated only 15,000 temporary residents. The Home Owners Loan Corporation (HOLC) lent money to impoverished mortgagors to guarantee the existence of the family home. Another alphabet agency, the Farm Security Administration (FSA), tried to block the exodus of farmers from their midwestern homes by providing long-term loans at low interest and by sponsoring cooperative buying. In 1937 Congress passed the Wagner-Steagall Act, directly subsidizing public housing projects with federal grants. But even then, a cost-conscious Roosevelt saw such schemes as temporary relief measures, not permanent social reforms; fewer than 200,000 units were built before 1941, a tiny start toward decent homes for the urban poor. The president may have saved the middle class with emergency loans, but he could not be said to have embraced a welfare state. As a result, many Americans—especially the young, the poor, the elderly, and minority groups—struggled alone with their fears.

The Young, the Old, and Racial Minorities

Expectations, often raised in the 1920s, were cruelly frustrated in the 1930s. In particular, education, historically the key to upward social mobility in the United States, changed course during the depression years. Once melting pots for an Americanizing culture or preparatory schools for university training, high schools came to emphasize "education for life." Social adjustment and skill in some trade seemed more appropriate for the times than academic subjects. After high school most rural graduates stayed on the family farm, took jobs—when they could—in small towns, or drifted toward the cities. Only war brought permanent, full-time work as soldiers or factory workers. About a quarter of America's adolescents went on to college, usually matriculating in a local or state-supported school. Students shunned the ballyhoo frivolities of the 1920s, faculties everywhere commenting on their increased seriousness. Most collegians eschewed business careers—no one talked about that "first million" anymore—and trained instead for a secure job, perhaps in government. The New Deal helped poor students with special work programs and even allowed some to go on federal relief rolls. But persistent depression meant that about one in three graduates took jobs for which they were "over-trained."

The nation's educational system stood the strain of economic crisis better than many other institutions, though some small colleges closed for lack of money in 1933 and 1934. Universities with larger endowments actually profited from deflation, and some made wise investments that assured their future eminence. On the public school level literacy was almost an American birthright, so despite huge losses in tax revenue—about a third less than predepression levels—most districts, at least outside the South, kept schoolhouse doors open. Teachers on fixed incomes at first benefited from the decline in prices, and when enrollment slipped late in the decade, spread-the-work schemes (whereby school boards dismissed teachers whose husbands were employed) still ensured a living wage. As more and more secondary schools and teacher training colleges took up John Dewey's theories of self-motivation and "learning by doing," the debate over curriculum rekindled itself. Critics like Robert Hutchins of the University of Chicago belabored "the loss of cultural and spiritual values" and wanted to return to a classical education based upon the "great books" of Western civilization. Leading universities, including Columbia and Chicago, experimented with such prescriptions; their traditionalist texts, however, too often emphasized authoritarian philosophies and ignored technology, the fine arts, and new disciplines like sociology and psychology. Hutchins's theories gradually died out, particularly after his attacks on "subsidized athletics" angered alumni. But a few schools, like St John's of Annapolis, refined his ideas about curriculum into permanent courses of study.

Americans also tinkered with new ways to help another segment of the population, the elderly. Depression had turned the placid retirement years of many senior citizens into a frightening time of uncertainty. Savings had evaporated in market panics and bank closings, while jobs for older workers were almost nonexistent. Worries about ill health and the "poor house" often made the elderly vulnerable to demagogic panaceas. Francis E. Townsend mesmerized audiences with his "old age revolving pension." The plan, though fiscally impossible, intrigued some 5 million Americans who joined "Townsend Clubs." Partly because of the obvious needs of the elderly and their no less obvious political clout, Roosevelt fashioned a relief program for them which was passed by an enthusiastic Congress. Under this Social Security Act a married couple received about $55 a month, enough to ease the worst anxieties and to ensure a basic standard of living. Washington also matched state grants for the blind, the crippled, and mothers with dependent children.

Although the New Deal helped America's young people and brought a small measure of security to its older folk, it frustrated the hopes of the nation's racial minorities. Cosmetic reforms toward an integrated society scarcely alleviated social bigotry and economic discrimination. The

Supreme Court chipped away at the "separate but equal" doctrine, demanding that southern school districts provide an education of equal quality for both races—a monetary impossibility during depression since . black schools required massive upgrading. Roosevelt appointed several blacks to middle-level administration posts, and in 1929 Oscar DePriest of Chicago had become the first black man since Reconstruction to sit in the House of Representatives. But when both Lou Henry Hoover and Eleanor Roosevelt invited Mrs DePriest to tea at the White House,

southern legislatures condemned the First Ladies for entertaining Negroes on a parity with whites, and neither president took the opportunity to challenge southern bigotry. They also ignored Senate filibusters against anti-lynching bills, and Roosevelt exempted farm workers—mostly southern blacks—from Social Security coverage, and maintained racial segregation in most federal enterprises.

On the other hand, Presidents Hoover and Roosevelt each gave some attention to the problems of blacks. Herbert Hoover repeatedly asked for black representatives to various conferences called to improve housing or health standards. He greatly increased government support of all-black Howard University in Washington DC, and in several other ways gave tangible support to black welfare. Franklin Roosevelt perhaps had a keener understanding of black privations and is often credited with making great progress in behalf of blacks. But much of the improvement has to do with rhetoric and symbol or the sheer activity of government or simply the advancing years. This was adequate, however, by 1936 to pull the black community away from its Republican moorings for the first time in history.

Roosevelt appointed two men, one white and one black, to oversee treatment of blacks in the New Deal agencies. And many blacks did find improved and more numerous employment opportunities in the new federal bureaucracy in Washington DC. But in the heavy majority of cases, the various New Deal agencies deferred to local custom in granting jobs and determining living conditions. The Tennessee Valley Authority set up all-white model towns and left blacks to live in shacks. The NRA was particularly offensive, permitting blacks to be paid less than whites for equal work and granting skilled jobs almost wholly to whites. Roosevelt was a symbol for all human aspirations including those of blacks, but he was clearly not an activist in the cause of black welfare. He followed the advice of southerners on his staff and rarely spoke out for blacks. Eleanor Roosevelt partially compensated for presidential inaction by including black and unsegregated audiences on her itineraries, welcoming mixed racial groups at the White House, and speaking up for blacks at key points. When the Daughters of the American Revolution refused to allow Marian Anderson to sing in Constitution Hall, for example, Mrs Roosevelt secured permission to hold the concert at the Lincoln Memorial.

Worse than this political neglect, economic adversity once again demonstrated that blacks were "last hired, first fired." In 1931, the Department of Labor reported

"Last hired, first fired," was proved again for blacks in the depression. Georgia Jungle *by Alexander Brook depicts the squalor he found "right in the heart of America."*

that Chicago had a black population constituting 4 per cent of its citizenry, but 16 per cent of the total unemployed; in Pittsburgh, 8 per cent of the population and 38 per cent of the unemployed were black; and in Memphis, Negroes were 38 per cent of the population and 75 per cent of the unemployed.

Long oppressed by Dixie's system of informal terror, southern blacks acquiesced, but urban minorities in the North fought back against racism which compounded the trials of depression. Blacks picketed ghetto stores that refused to hire black employees, and "Buy Black" campaigns erupted in New York, New Jersey, and Illinois. Race hatred culminated in 1935 when rumors that a store manager had beaten a little black boy to death for stealing a penknife set off almost a week of rioting in New York's Harlem. Three blacks died, 200 more of both races were injured, including policemen, and property damage reached into the millions. The riot spurred interest in sects like the Black Muslims, founded five years earlier by W. D. Fard. During the mid-1930s, the movement's great organizer, known as Elijah Muhammad, proclaimed the "inherent evil of all white devils" and charted a course toward outright separatism. Rejecting completely "the white society of oppression," Muhammad preached that "a new dignity of self-denial will revive the power of the black race." The 1930s fit easily into the long pattern of racial hostilities in American history.

That the American Indian shared the problems of blacks was certainly not the fault of President Herbert Hoover, who had a strong personal interest in Indian welfare. Two of his uncles had worked as Indian agents. Added to Hoover's interest in the West and his awareness of the Quaker tradition of fair treatment to Indians, this perhaps accounts for his care in selecting a Quaker, Charles J. Rhoads, to replace the racist Hubert Work, who described Indians as "primitive, nomadic people without . . . social or political entity. . . ." Rhoads, who for years served as treasurer of the Indian Rights Association, and his new assistant, J. Henry Scattergood, were Philadelphia bankers noted for their leadership in charitable work.

The government under Hoover adhered to no simple plan of assimilation, which could have indicated contempt for Indian culture, or of the reservation plan, which could spell permanent segregation. Under Rhoads and Scattergood the Indian Bureau held to the traditional Jeffersonian-Progressive goal of assimilating the Indians into American society. But Hoover in 1930 wanted to "blend them as a self-supporting people into the nation as a whole" without sacrificing the unique Indian culture.

The Indian Bureau under Hoover actually ended up with a mixture of the two philosophies. It encouraged native arts and crafts, along with modern skills such as auto mechanics. Hoover even wanted a permanent record made of Indian sign languages. Rhoads and Scattergood,

astute conservationists, worried about the loss or corruption of traditional skills even as they embraced the melting pot ideal. They were essentially transition figures. Under Rhoads permanent employment of Indians by the bureau increased substantially. Interested in preserving the Indian family, Rhoads endorsed Senator Charles McNary's Klamath tribal incorporation bill, which in the sociologist John Collier's words "marked a great historical change in Indian policy." But Rhoads shrank from a general application of this principle; he still wanted to force the white man's culture on the Indian.

Perhaps the most creditable accomplishment for Indians in the Hoover administration came in simple budgetary terms. In spite of the increase in appropriations throughout the decade, the Interior Department report of 1927 entitled one section "The Poverty of the Indian Service." Between 1929 and 1932 Indian expenditures almost doubled, rising from $16 to $27 million. This increase—an initial $3 million request and a deficiency appropriation settled on in 1929 and a 30 per cent

Forced onto reservations and then neglected, Indians had only their innate dignity to fall back on. Above: An old Indian squaw and a young child are portrayed by an inquiring white man's camera. Right: Flathead Indians of Glacier National Park sit outside their tepees in varying garb in 1936. Inset: The proud image of Chief Two Guns appeared on the old Buffalo Nickel.

increase effective in the next fiscal year—escaped the fierce economizing after the crash because Hoover knew Indian conditions to be deplorable. Most of the funds went for schools and hospitals, better food, and clothing for Indian children.

Under Franklin Roosevelt an Indian Reorganization Bill, passed as the Wheeler Act of 1934, gave central importance to the Indian tribe and the preservation of varied Indian cultures. Drafted by John Collier, the new law restored tribal self-government and rejected the movement toward assimilation. Yet the Indian remained in an abject state, as this 1935 government report amply shows:

> The three outstanding disease problems among the Indians today are tuberculosis, trachoma, and intestinal disorders of infancy. The acute infectious diseases of childhood, notably measles and whooping cough, are attended by a high mortality . . . . Skin diseases, particularly impetigo and ringworm, are extremely common among children and a source of considerable complaint from the school authorities.

> The diet of most tribes is not balanced and is deficient in many respects. Such articles as milk and fresh vegetables are used very seldom or not at all. . . . Malnutrition is reported by agency physicians to be fairly common among the children; on the other hand overweight due to the excessive carbohydrate diet may be seen quite frequently in adults . . . . The house itself may be built of clay, reeds, stones, or logs found in the immediate vicinity, or it may be a simple cabin constructed of wrought lumber. These primitive abodes do not afford reasonable protection from the elements. Overcrowding is extremely common. . . . There is scarcely any separation of ordinary functions such as cooking, living, and sleeping; privacy is out of the question. Water for drinking purposes often is polluted with domestic sewage. In much of the Indian country, the supply of water is very limited and must be transported some distance, thus personal and household cleanliness is rendered difficult even if the Indian were so inclined. . . . The great majority of Indian homes use a surface type of privy or, as so frequently happens, they have no methods of excreta disposal. . . . Improvements of the Indian's physical surroundings remains a problem to be solved if diseases associated with defective environment are to be controlled.

An old dilemma about race—bigotry toward neighbors, charity for strangers safely removed—reasserted itself during these same years. Most Americans reacted with outrage toward the persecution of Jews in Nazi Germany. Although the Ku Klux Klan had launched antisemitic campaigns in America during the 1920s like those pro-Nazi

groups pursued in the 1930s, Hitler's pogroms and discriminatory laws angered Americans and provoked protests from the Roosevelt administration as early as 1933. The Committee on Displaced Scholars and other groups attracted European Jewish intellectuals to American universities, museums, and cultural centers. Although poorly paid for their services in this period, the Jewish elite—in contrast to ordinary Jews who were cruelly denied entry—found haven in America, thanks to a clause in the immigration laws favoring educated foreigners. From 1933 to 1944 Jews made up one-third of all immigrants and well over half of the refugees. Most sought to escape religious and racial persecution after they had gone from country to country in Europe, fleeing Hitler's advances. Most of the art scholars who left Germany, for instance, did so when German laws, beginning in 1933, left them jobless because of their Jewish descent. The thousands of German and Central European intellectuals—artists, scholars, and scientists (notably Albert Einstein)—who escaped persecution in the 1930s formed the largest single cultural migration to America for at least a century.

In 1935 after the Nazis organized particularly brutal attacks against German Jews, the president recalled America's ambassador, Hugh Wilson—an unmistakable act of condemnation. But the State Department, worried about international politics, blocked proposals to liberalize immigration quotas to admit more Jewish refugees. Then, too, popular opinion at home worried more about overseas bigotry than about widespread antisemitism in America itself. Jews were discriminated against in housing and jobs and suffered social exclusion. Though Ivy League law schools, for example, angrily denied that they had a "non-Christian" admissions quota, every year almost exactly 10 per cent of entering classes were Jewish.

Beating the Blues

Despite disheartening failures, the 1930s were not years of unrelieved gloom. With so much uncertainty around, people invented a panoply of ways to escape, to forget the present. Roosevelt's busy New Deal never solved the depression riddle of poverty amid abundance, so many Americans sought ways to ignore the problems surrounding them. Any fads or bizarre acts that temporarily got rid of the blues quickly gained nationwide attention.

Parlor games changed to meet the need and the opportunity for inexpensive, readily available entertainment. Card playing, especially the new game of contract bridge, became immensely popular. After Ely Culbertson and his wife beat Sidney Lenz and Oswald Jacoby in a 150-game "Battle of the Century" on radio, over 20 million people

*Radio had the ability to reach into every home.
Above: The month-long radio and newspaper publicity
given to the victory (by 8,980 points) of
Ely Culbertson and his wife over Sidney Lenz
(center) and Oswald Jacoby made contract bridge
a fad all over America. Right: Popular Kate
Smith belts out a song on the radio in 1935.*

learned the ''Culbertson system'' of point count and bid-
ding. Other crazes—jigsaw puzzles, Monopoly, Ping Pong
—occupied the leisure moments of millions more during
the depression.

For American stay-at-homes the most ubiquitous entertainment came over the air waves. The number of radio
sets quadrupled during the decade to over 40 million.
Dance music from New York City nightclubs or popular
singers like Kate Smith filled many hours, but most
popular of all was comedy. After all, what was more
needed? Yet radio changed Americans in ways they perhaps did not fully realize. As it broadcast big league
contests and Broadway show tunes, radio did much to
homogenize the nation, to create universal symbols.

Top: Underwood and Underwood. Bottom: The Bettmann Archive

Outside the home, bingo games, slot machines, pinball boards, and prize contests offered a chance to win something for very little. A lucky bingo card often selling for only a penny might win a ham or a new shirt. Slot machines, then legal throughout most of the country except the East Coast, returned 75 cents on each dollar, one of the few games which offered money rewards. Thousands danced on weekends in local "hippodromes" to the sounds of swing music—happy tunes with a quick beat—made famous by Benny Goodman. Doing the "Big Apple" or the "Lambeth Walk" under twirling specks of light reflected overhead from hundreds of little mirrors calmed worries about the next paycheck.

Nationwide Trends

Something more than technology homogenized the nation. Depression itself forced America into physical similarity. Big corporations, much more than local shopkeepers, had access to credit and could take advantage of the intricacies of government regulation. As prices declined, eastern executives bought up brand names at bargain levels; another age would give the name conglomerates to the sprawling enterprises that resulted. The economics of large-scale production forced many local craftsmen out of business, unable to compete in a mass market.

Supplied by a few giant factories, chain stores began to refashion Main Street into that sameness which would characterize the later twentieth century. Clothing styles responded more to the profit sheets of distant garment centers than to the needs of local climate. During January and February, for example, people in the Gulf States could purchase new overcoats but—at least in many stores—not short-sleeve shirts. Canned goods more than ever wiped out seasonal or regional menus. Even differences in local government blurred as Washington replaced them as the source of policy and money. Citizens became adept at dealing with bureaucracies that made few distinctions.

Folk heroes reminded people of their humanity or distracted them from anxiety. Will Rogers, the Oklahoma cowboy humorist famous in the twenties, continued making prickly observations about political figures. "I only know what I read in the papers," he told audiences, "so sometimes I feel like the most educated man in Washington." Action mingled with gaiety in Fiorello LaGuardia, mayor of New York City. First elected in 1933 on a fusion ticket backed by liberals and Republicans, LaGuardia defeated challenges from a corrupt Tammany Hall discredited by former Mayor Jimmy Walker's excesses.

A long-time friend of organized labor, "the Little Flower" delivered twelve years of non partisan, honest government. Public works, especially bridges and high-

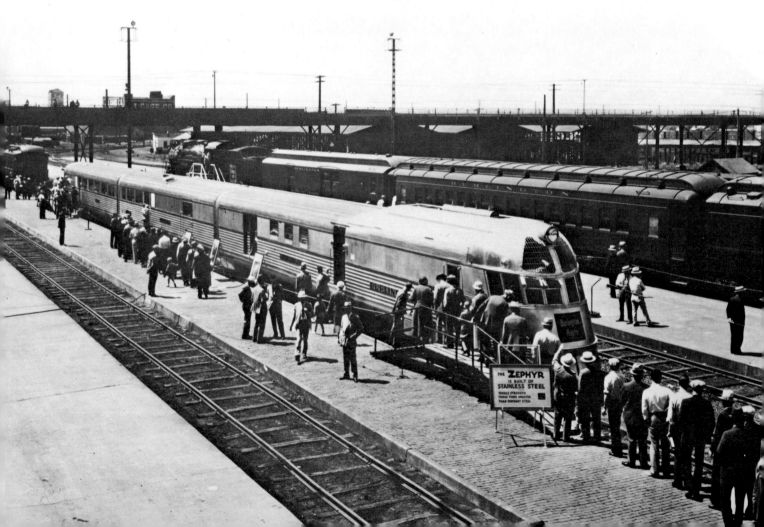

Below left: The tour of the new Burlington Zephyr marked the transformation of the railroads from steam locomotion and bulky carriages to diesel and streamlined stainless steel. Right: During the depression, Americans flocked in larger numbers than usual to recreation parks, beaches, and sports events. This photograph shows golfers on the WPA links at Rock Creek Park, Illinois.

US Parks Department

ways, low-cost housing, and new city parks, together with efficient social welfare agencies transformed New York into the nation's most progressive city. LaGuardia's humanitarian humor won widespread affection. He read the comics to New York's children over the radio, often explaining their subtleties. During a coal strike, he turned off the heat in the room where the operators and miners had deadlocked. When diplomats from Nazi Germany visited Manhattan, he assigned only Jewish policemen to their official escort.

If Americans drifted into dreams, they also took up more physical pastimes. Depression accelerated an earlier trend toward more and more free time; the country still spent about 10 per cent of its national income on vacationing and recreation. Even more than the new streamlined trains with air-conditioned Pullman cars, the country's highways took people to inexpensive vacation spots such as national parks and sea shores. Automobile ownership actually increased during the 1930s as low fuel costs and the appearance of inexpensive tourist camps and cabins enticed millions onto the roads. Auto trailers also began to appear in large numbers. Enforced leisure revived the recreation movement begun some thirty years earlier by employers anxious to provide wholesome activity for their workers. The Works Progress Administration (WPA) spent huge amounts on local parks, swimming pools, tennis courts, and beaches. State efforts also contributed to the nearly $1 billion lavished on new recreation areas. In New York State, for example, Robert Moses opened for public use miles of bathing beaches on Long Island and built roads and bridges to reach them. Admission to pools alone surpassed the annual attendance at all spectator

sports. Hard times revolutionized sedentary habits. The public spent four times as much money engaging in amateur sports as it did on watching professional contests. Depression weakened the popularity of football, of necessity a costly amusement, though some teams took advantage of cheap labor to erect enormous stadiums, such as the new Yale Bowl, built to hold 55,000. Apart from the new game of softball, the most popular pursuits —swimming, golf—reflected a tendency away from family-oriented recreation toward individualized games.

Nothing illustrated this shift better than America's discovery of winter sports, especially skiing and figure skating. Before the 1930s downhill skiing, dependent upon a particular combination of climate and terrain, and requiring specialized equipment, was not widely pursued. Cross country skiing, well known in ski country, was more a practical than a sporting consideration. Then the 1932 Winter Olympics, held in Lake Placid, New York, exposed Americans to expert skiing which, aided by inexpensive railroad fares, started a national craze. Soon European instructors coaxed thousands down the slopes of fashionable resorts in such states as Vermont, New York, Colorado and Idaho. Then a figure skater, Sonja Henie, began her professional career in 1936 after winning three successive gold medals in international competitions. The beautiful Norwegian's annual tours and many films created a widespread interest in figure skating and ice carnivals.

The public often fastened upon sports heroes during the 1930s, seemingly more interested by individual achievement than by team efforts. The sports hero of the decade was the black boxer Joe Louis. Son of an Alabama

73

The "Iron Horse," Lou Gehrig, only faltered after 2,130 consecutive games when he contracted a fatal illness. Right: Saying goodbye on his last day as a Yankee in 1939. Left: Joe Louis defeats Max Schmeling in 1938. The "Brown Bomber" defended the world heavyweight crown twenty-five times before he retired undefeated in 1949. Below left: One of the greatest track athletes of all time, Jesse Owens competes in the long jump. Below: Owens breasts the tape to win the 100 meter dash in 10.3 seconds at the 1936 Berlin Olympics.

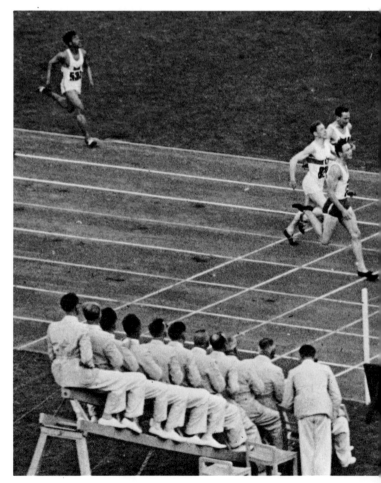

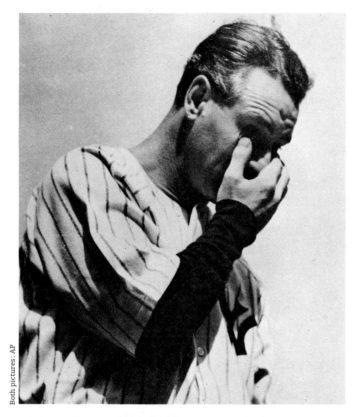

Both pictures: AP

sharecropper, the "Brown Bomber" turned pro in 1934, defeating former heavyweight champion Max Baer that same year. Millions followed his career on the radio as he won bout after bout, losing only to Max Schmeling, the great German fighter. In 1937, only three years after his debut, Louis knocked out James Braddock for the world championship. The next year, wanting to revenge his earlier defeat, Louis again met Schmeling. Patriotic Americans, and especially blacks, hoped that he would humiliate the white man who Hitler bragged had proved Nazi theories about a master race of Aryans. Louis destroyed Schmeling in the first round, forever ensuring himself a prominent niche in America's sports pantheon. Nor could any Nordic run so fast as the black Jesse Owens in the world Olympics held in Germany in 1936.

The bad economy severely restricted most team sports, especially the most popular new game of the 1920s, college football. Declining enrolments together with great expense confined football to heavily endowed private schools and big state universities. Yet promoters quickly sensed the potential profits in end-of-the-season matches between major winners. By the mid-1930s, over fifty "bowls," named after fruits, flowers, or local crops, lured fans and teams to the South for annual contests. The most famous game, played in 1934 at the grandfather of arenas, the Rose Bowl in Pasadena, California, pitted the All American Indians of Stanford against Columbia University's Lions. Sportswriters haughtily dismissed "the nice little Eastern team," but Lions coach Lou Little concentrated on defense while Stanford players planned victory celebrations. Columbia quarterback Al Barabas ran a "spinner," surprising Stanford backs with a seventeen-yard touchdown run around the "wrong" end in the second quarter; spectacular goal line stands prevented the Indians from scoring. The 7–0 Columbia victory, perhaps the most stunning upset in Rose Bowl history, marked a subtle shift in collegiate football. More and more coaches relentlessly drilled players motivated as much by future professional careers as by school spirit. Professionalization also affected college basketball. Schools like Kentucky University and North Carolina State built huge stadiums, launched nationwide recruiting hunts, and competed at National Invitational Tournaments for yearly championships.

These dramatic changes did not affect America's favorite sport, baseball, perhaps because it had always been a business. The New York Yankees dominated the American League throughout the thirties, winning six pennants and five World Series contests. The Yanks always had a certain style. During the 1932 Series, for example, an aging Babe Ruth (he would retire in three years) sauntered to home plate and grandly pointed to center field—where two pitches later he hit a home run! The great Yankee manager, Joe McCarthy, and players like Lou Gehrig and Joe DiMaggio led fans to chant, "How

Moral Re-Armament

Moral Re-Armament was described by its founder as an "expeditionary force from all faiths and races . . . to modernize the character and purpose of man." Above: A parade in San Francisco, 1939.

much are we gonna win by today?" but consistent victories dulled interest in a team and sport that seemed to manufacture wins on an assembly line. In the "other league" the colorful Gas-House Gang of St Louis Cardinals bragged outrageously at press conferences and cavorted on the field. The leader of the "swashbuckling Cards," Dizzy Dean, delighted fans with witty comments about politicians, baseball rivals, whatever came to mind.

Many Americans did not try to escape depression by transfering their hopes to larger-than-life sports idols or submerging their anxieties in the momentary excitement of team competitions. Instead, they took up religion. Rheinhold Niebuhr attracted intellectuals with the argument that the calamities of depression and world war showed man's apostasy in daring to guide his own affairs. Only a return to more primitive ideas about man's depravity and his utter dependence upon God's mercy could ensure society's salvation. At the same time, popularizers spread fundamentalism or proclaimed new cults. Father Divine, a black evangelist in Harlem, called his followers "angels" and organized religious communes as "heavens." Many thought that he was God in black skin and praised him for his job placement services and free soup kitchens. White cultists found in Jehovah's Witnesses that apocalyptic vision which made economic adversity understandable. Jesus would soon return to establish His kingdom on earth; only those who had "witnessed" their faith would survive Armageddon. Still, most Americans avoided radical religion. During the 1930s, church membership and attendance declined steadily. The rootlessness and uncertainty which characterized all Americans in the thirties had aroused doubt about the faith of their fathers. As a college boy put it to the sociologists Robert and Helen Lynd: "I believe these things, but they don't take a large place in my life."

Though Americans for the most part ignored other-worldly concerns, depression popularized movements which promised spiritual awakening or practical moral-ity. The Oxford Group, founded in England shortly after the First World War by Frank Buchman, a Lutheran mini-ster from America, fed on the uncertainty of the 1930s, becoming the Atlantic community's most fashionable evangelical movement. Buchman preached a simple system of ethics rooted in the "Four Absolutes" of honesty, purity, unselfishness, and love. Believers medi-tated daily, usually in early morning, seeking "guidance" and gathered at "house-parties." The Oxford Group's sketchy dreams of a cooperative Christian commonwealth fascinated many wealthy or well-educated with hopes for a more ethical future less dependent on Rooseveltian experiments. Especially after Buchman angrily attacked "godless communism" in Soviet Russia, Manhattan matrons and earnest Ivy Leaguers proselytized privately among their peers and publicly at much-ballyhoed World

Assemblies. When Europe drifted toward war and totalitarianism in the late thirties, Buchman renamed his movement Moral Re-Armament. Only a "God-controlled" world could ensure peace, economic security and liberty.

Hopes for the Future

Despite the comforts some drew from religion, sports, and parlor games, an unnerving sense of decline still afflicted the daily lives of most citizens. A fitting epitaph for the depression years might be the strange juxtaposition of ritualized crime and gaudy world fairs. Each somehow obliquely reassured Americans. The ending of prohibition and the onset of hard times halved the revenue from organized crime. Predictably enough, crimes against property (like stealing or "con games") increased dramatically during the thirties, as did arrests for vagrancy and drunkenness. But personal assaults declined. More surprisingly, an old American type re-

Bonnie Parker and Clyde Barrow robbed and killed their way through Missouri, Texas, and Oklahoma for the excitement as much as anything else. They taunted police by posturing in photos (below) and posting them to the press.

Both pictures: Brown Brothers

appeared, the bandit or outlaw who panicked whole regions with sprees of violent revenge against society. Some, like Clyde Barrow and his "moll" Bonnie, were pathetic people too buffeted by depression and ignorance to understand why they compulsively, happily robbed banks and killed. John Dillinger, in contrast, reveled in his notoriety as J. Edgar Hoover's "Public Enemy Number One." Federal agents or state police staged elaborate ambushes of such figures, gunning down Dillinger outside a movie theater in Chicago and brutally assassinating the Barrow gang along back roads in Oklahoma. Newspapers headlined the violent careers of such bandits and the American people took solace, it seemed, from their tragic examples. The average man may have worried about his job, but he was not a crook.

Americans dreamed of a better future. Twenty million

The 1930s saw an outbreak of gangsterism with thugs like "Pretty Boy" Floyd, "Machine Gun" Kelly, and John Dillinger. After Dillinger was slain by federal agents in 1934, his body was displayed in the County Morgue at Chicago.

people visited the "Century of Progress" exposition in Chicago during 1933–34 to stare at the gadgetry of technology and wonder about the possibilities of science. Others clambered over a huge reconstructed Mayan Temple or watched the fan dances of stripper Sally Rand. Five years later an even more ambitious undertaking, the Golden Gate International Exposition at San Francisco, looked to a future of swift transportation and almost simultaneous communication. Ironically enough, the 400-acre pageant took as its theme, "Recreation— Man's Gift from a Machine Age." But the papier-mâché fantasies culminated with the giant New York World's Fair of 1939. Nearly 50 million people strolled around the "Trylon and Perisphere"—a 728-foot needle pyramid and a 180-foot globe—which symbolized "The World of Tomorrow." The bold, modern architecture was neither classical nor Gothic. There everyone could feel himself a part of progress again. Huge exhibits portrayed a future built around cooperation and the rational use of resources. Such earnest hopes, belied by the beginning of yet another war among the great powers, symbolized the paradoxes inflicted upon the victims of depression.

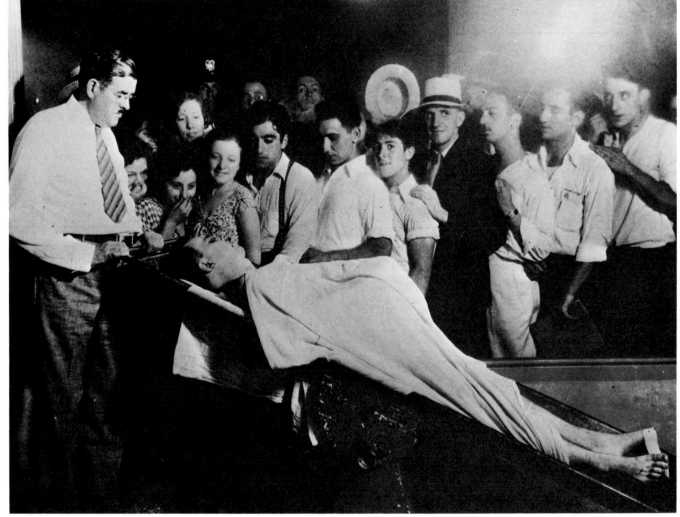

Chapter 4

ART, ANGER, AND ESCAPE

As America sought to rescue and rebuild her damaged society, her artists—writers, painters, musicians, showmen— provided both a mirror of depression and a bromide of escapism. Literature witnessed the new realism of James T. Farrell and John Steinbeck, as well as a great outpouring of lush period romance. The fine arts experienced the same trends, from the bleak hardness of Grant Wood to the bucolic realism of Thomas Hart Benton. Popular music and films showed a particular bent for extravagance and escape, while serious theater disdained fantasy in favor of ideas. The threadbare existence of many Americans in the depression was relieved by the intellectual stimulus, the glamor, and the humor earnestly produced by the nation's creative artists.

Culture in the Thirties

Nothing in American life was untouched by the Great Depression. This was certainly true of the nation's artists, writers, musicians, and providers of entertainment in the theater, motion pictures, and radio. Some found that their money had run out, or that other people no longer had money to back their projects. Some lost their jobs and had to cast about for other work. A good many writers and painters had been living in Europe. Most of these expatriates were obliged to come home. In common with other Americans, they tried to understand what had happened. In general, they had not taken politics seriously during the 1920s. Now the very fabric of their nation was in question. In the past, said the poet Archibald MacLeish, "America was promises." Had the promises turned out to be false? With millions on relief and factories closed or on short time, was capitalism doomed? If so, was communism the answer? If not, how could the United States be put on its feet? How could the truth of American experience be rendered by the creative imagination? How could the arts contribute? Ought they to be vehicles of protest and propaganda? Or was the public more in need of uplift, amusement, distraction? Which was better? For Hollywood and Broadway the problem had to be posed in cash terms. Which would bring the audiences, a somber portrayal of hard times or some light-hearted piece of "escapism"? Was it possible to combine the two, by admitting that things were bad but facing up cheerfully to them? "Brother, Can You Spare A Dime?" was one song of the early depression with a grim message. "Who's Afraid of the Big Bad Wolf?" was a much more cheerful ditty—more popular and perhaps more wholesome.

No single solution was ever agreed upon. Art was turned both to anger and to escape. Occasionally it sought to combine entertainment values (a good story, possibly a catchy tune) with what was often called "social significance." What was produced, in all its variety, is important not only for its own merit but because it is our chief way of getting into the American mind of the 1930s. Much of the "truth" of the depression years is strangely irrecoverable. Statistics and speeches are apt to go dead. To get the feel of the depression we must pay attention to its good dreams and bad dreams, and the people who articulated them.

First, the writers and artists. In the autumn of 1932 fifty-three well-known intellectuals explained in an open letter why they recommended support for the Communist party in the forthcoming presidential election. Certain of them, including Clifton Fadiman and Sherwood Anderson, also testified to their political reawakening in the radical magazine *New Masses.* This journal, which had been struggling along with a tiny circulation since 1926,

became the focus of Communist or pro-Communist writing under the vigorous direction of Mike Gold. In the closing days of the Hoover administration and at the start of the New Deal, Marxist ideas had a quite strong appeal for American intellectuals. They tended to feel that neither the Republicans nor the Democrats, nor the native American Socialist party, went to the root of the nation's difficulties. They criticized America for the gulf between rich and poor, and for indifference to the arts. They criticized themselves for previous self-indulgence. The 1920s had been the era of the "lost generation." The 1930s, it was said, was the era of the "crisis generation." One could not opt out by catering to the tastes of rich patrons or retreating into the bohemianism of Parisian café life. "Bourgeois" was a dirty word in the new vocabulary. Some of America's writers and artists identified with the "workers" or the "proletariat." They tried to depict the existences of hoboes, sharecroppers, jobless men, trade unionists. They hoped to speak *to* as well as *for* such citizens. Mike Gold appealed to the workers themselves to contribute to his magazine.

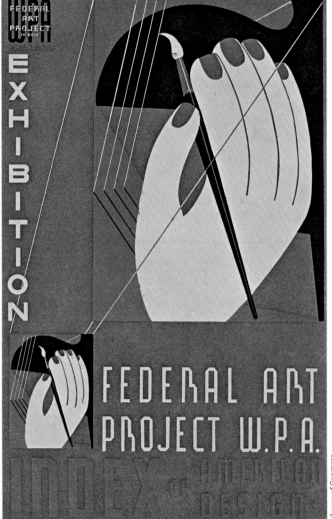

Work Projects Administration/National Archives

Index of American Design. National Gallery of Art, Washington

Through the WPA and other New Deal agencies, painters, photographers, and writers obtained work from the federal government. Left: A poster produced by the WPA publicises the Index of American Design, *the designs for which have been recognized as folk art themselves. Above: A rare coverlet is reproduced for insertion in the* Index. *Right: A fine illustration of a circus wagon which appeared in the catalog.*

To some extent this mood of emotional radicalism persisted through the 1930s. It was revived during the Spanish Civil War of 1936–39, when Russia supported the Spanish government and Hitler and Mussolini backed the right-wing rising led by General Franco. At the time these sympathies were attacked by many Americans as either subversive or silly. After the Second World War old manifestoes were to be dug up and indicted by congressional and state committees on un-American activities. But at the time they were not illegal and not surprising. Even conservative Americans admitted that the country was in a terrible mess.

The main feature of American culture in the depression years is not the tinge of radicalism, but the failure of extreme ideas to win any wide following. And the main reason is that creative talent remained basically individual. American writers and artists might wish to express solidarity with the workers. But after all, most of them had never regarded themselves as gentlemen or aesthetes. There was an old American tradition on which the 1930s could build—the creator as ordinary American, even in his way as an American patriot. Moreover, the emphasis on individual freedom of expression collided with the totalitarian aspects of Stalinist Russia. So the angry manifestoes of 1932–33, interpreted in this light, have little in common with the dutiful rhetoric of Old World communism. The first issue of a raucous little magazine, *Americana* (November 1932),

edited by Gilbert Seldes and others, announced that ''our civilization exudes a miasmic stench'' and that ''we had better prepare to give it a decent but rapid burial.'' They described themselves as ''laughing morticians.'' But they also declared themselves as ''unconditionally opposed to Comrade Stalin and his federal bureaucracy in Moscow.'' This was the spirit of such contributors as the novelist Nathanael West and the humorist S. J. Perelman.

Sentimental preferences for communism were weakened by the revelations of rigged trials in Russia, and by the shock of the Nazi-Soviet pact in 1939. But domestic factors were more crucial. The WPA and various other New Deal agencies found work for thousands of creative talents. Writers compiled guidebooks of cities and states. Folk songs were recorded in remote corners of the Union. So were the reminiscences of old Negroes who had been born into slavery. Photographers, among them the incomparably honest Walker Evans, caught forever the passing moments of commonplace travail. Painters with modest official commissions daubed murals on innumerable post office walls throughout the land. Other artists collaborated to compile an Index of American Design. Their careful rendering of artefacts ranging from colonial weather vanes to old-fashioned phonographs itself became a new form of folk art. For a few years the Federal Theater Project aroused a similar spirit of experiment and recollection among stage professionals.

Above: Daughters of Revolution *by Grant Wood.*
The painting is a wry response to the prim
indignation of the DAR, who were incensed when Wood
chose to execute a work commissioned by them
in Germany rather than the United States.

The most famous writers and artists could survive without regular government patronage. Of the total amount of literature and art produced in the decade only a small proportion was the result of federal commissions. Of the federally inspired work, as critics hastened to point out, some was mediocre. Nevertheless, this patronage met some needs that went far beyond winning votes among the highbrows for Franklin D. Roosevelt. It was attuned to the psychological mood of the nation. Sensitive Americans were worried by the extent of hardship and injustice. They were inclined to blame big business for the waste of human and natural resources. Yet for many the depression involved a rediscovery of America. In part it was an actual, physical discovery—of places and regions they had never really looked at. In part it was a spiritual homecoming—a realization that they loved their country in spite of or even because of its faults.

This complex response, anger and affection, is apparent in much of the painting of the 1930s. There is a satirical element, for instance, in the work of the Iowa-born Grant Wood, as in his *Daughters of Revolution* or his *American Gothic.* Wood's Americans are hard and prim. But they are not weak, and they keep their Iowa farm landscapes in beautiful order. Approval of the prairie pioneers is still clearer in the paintings of

John Steuart Curry. Curry's homesteaders have to struggle to win a livelihood. Their lives are bleak and lonely. But he evidently admires them. Thomas Hart Benton, a third painter of middle-western scenes, had, like Wood and Curry, studied in Paris before avowedly returning to his own region of his own country. "No American art," he said in 1932, "can come to those who do not live an American life, who do not have an American psychology, and who cannot find in America justification of their lives." Benton painted swirling canvases, peopled with gnarled, hectic characters—sharecroppers, Negroes, figures from the past such as the abolitionist John Brown. His was a gallery of American victims and heroes, comparable to the potted biographies in the trilogy *USA* (1936) by the novelist John Dos Passos.

Wood, Curry, and Benton were "regionalists" who disliked big cities and on the whole preferred to paint a bygone America. Other artists such as Charles Sheeler and Edward Hopper had already established their styles before the depression came. Sheeler was fascinated by shapes of buildings—first barns and silos, and then the clean abstract forms of industrial architecture. Hopper, too, loved buildings. But his particular feeling was for shabbiness and loneliness: frame houses with the paint peeling off, harshly lit streets almost empty of people, life at a tired standstill. Hopper was not a "depression"

Thomas Hart Benton's City Activities with Subway
(above right) was painted in 1930; Benton came to
specialize in rural subjects. Right: Edward
Hopper's Early Sunday Morning.

Above: John B. Flannagan's Triumph of the Egg
*(1937). The sculptor felt that "often there is
an occult attraction in the very shape of a
rock. . . ." Right:* Cradling Wheat *by Thomas Hart
Benton. As a leader of the regionalist movement,
Benton sought to recall pioneer America in a
nostalgic realism.*

painter; his themes did not essentially change over a
whole generation. The depression, rather, brought
together a mass of styles and theories, revealing each to
each in a fresh perspective. Thus the painters already
mentioned displayed a common awareness of the
American scene, and of sides of American life that were
peculiarly *American,* for better or worse. Such a feeling
might be deliberate or unconscious. It might be explicit
to the point of corniness, as with the big murals of Benton.
Or it might be hidden from the casual observer, as with
the abstract designs of Stuart Davis, who used "the
methods of modern French painting" to "paint what I see
in America." It might lead the artist to lyrical evocation of
country scenes; or to paint unemotionally like Sheeler, or
reticently like Hopper. It could embrace harsh satire, as
in some of the cartoons of William Gropper or the oil
paintings of Ben Shahn (notably his Sacco-Vanzetti series
of 1931–32). It made room also for the sleazy New York
street scenes of Reginald Marsh, and the sad, tortured
figures in the work of Philip Evergood. In sculpture it
included the fierce "medals of dishonor" conceived by
David Smith, and the beautiful animal figures carved in
wood or stone by John Flannagan. Flannagan, perhaps

86

Charles E. Burchfield's
November Evening *(opposite top) warns of an approaching storm. In* The Bowl *(opposite bottom), Reginald Marsh let his romantic imagination loose for a wild ride at Coney Island. Far from romantic is the starkly simple vision of Charles Sheeler's* American Landscape *(above). Edward Hopper usually preferred to tell a story of loneliness; he captured the dream world of the cinema in* New York Movie *(left).*

America's finest sculptural talent of the decade, was to die prematurely in 1942. Gaston Lachaise, the creator of superbly fleshy yet graceful figures of women, was America's other genius in sculpture. He died in 1935.

Each artist had his own unmistakable stamp. None responded to the depression through crude propaganda, except in a few murals that now look overblown. Each in his way was, however, affected by the depression. To the extent that this shattering experience revealed new depths in American life, things lying below the glossy surface, it drew forth an additional dimension.

Something of the same process is apparent in literature. The 1920s had been an era of dazzling innovation in fiction, theater, and poetry. The 1930s entailed a repudiation in some degree of earlier attitudes. Again, no neat diagram can be drawn. Thus, it would probably be agreed today that the two best American novelists living in the 1930s were William Faulkner and Ernest Hemingway. But neither was a depression novelist in any obvious sense. Faulkner was affected at the outset because his home town in Mississippi was flat broke, and he with it. He was therefore compelled to write for money, and to do some of this as a scriptwriter in Hollywood. Otherwise his fiction was not markedly influenced by the

Ernest Hemingway holds freshly caught trout in Sun Valley, Idaho, in 1939. The author-sportsman glorified an aggressively sophisticated world in his books.

The Bettmann Archive

circumstances of the decade. He continued to set his stories mostly in the South, and often in the past. By the mid-1930s he was relatively prosperous. Hemingway, on the strength of *A Farewell to Arms* (1929), was already famous. Apart from some short stories, Hemingway's chief writing in the early 1930s dealt with bullfighting in Spain and big game hunting in Africa. Not until 1937, with the publication of *To Have and Have Not,* did he produce a direct comment on the plight of the poor. Harry Morgan, the central character of the novel, has earned a reasonable income in Florida by renting his boat to wealthy fishermen. When this money dries up because of the depression, Morgan is forced into illegal and dangerous enterprises, one of which kills him. Morgan's dying message is: "One man alone ain't got . . . no chance." In other words, solidarity is necessary. The same idea is conveyed with greater length and complexity in Hemingway's novel of the Spanish Civil War, *For Whom the Bell Tolls* (1940). Hemingway took his title from a sermon by the English poet John Donne: "No man is an Island, entire of itself; every man is a piece of the Continent. . . . And therefore never send to know for whom the bell tolls; It tolls for thee."

For a strong "period" flavor we must look elsewhere than at Faulkner and Hemingway, especially at the novels written by their contemporary, John Dos Passos. *The 42nd Parallel, 1919,* and *The Big Money,* collected under the title *USA,* were all published in the 1930s, though they describe mainly the previous two decades. The trilogy is a remarkable mix of narrative, poetic personal reminiscence, and "documentary" (popular songs, news headlines, profiles of actual Americans such as Henry Ford and the newspaper tycoon William Randolph Hearst). In sheer technique *USA* is a brilliantly ingenious blend of fact and fiction. In mood it embodied the pessimistic cynicism of an author for whom mankind seemed to divide into cowardly crooks and courageous dupes. *USA*'s closing vignette is of a nameless "vag" (vagrant), trying to hitchhike across America. Luckier citizens pass high above him in a gleaming aircraft. He ponders their luxury, and the emptiness of the success slogans on which he was nourished: "Went to school, books said opportunity, ads promised speed, own your own home, shine bigger than your neighbor. . . ." Dos Passos continued his fictional panorama of hope and disillusion in *Adventures of a Young Man* (1939), which describes the ruthless opportunism of an American Communist organization. Then he yielded to another impulse. For a number of writers the rediscovery of America meant going back into the national heritage to draw comfort. Constance Rourke examined the tradition of *American Humor* (1931). Van Wyck Brooks, hitherto a highly skeptical chronicler of American literature, won a Pulitzer prize with *The Flowering of New England* (1936), an affectionate study of Emerson and Longfellow and

The Bettmann Archive

UPI

Brown Brothers

Three great novelists. John Dos Passos (left)
angrily examined industrial America in USA;
John Steinbeck (center) championed exploited
"forgotten men" in The Grapes of Wrath; *and*
William Faulkner (right) retreated into the
mythical county of Yoknapatawpha, Mississippi,
in books like The Sound and the Fury.

their literary kin. The poet Carl Sandburg toiled over a huge admiring biography of Abraham Lincoln. Sandburg also testified to his love of the average, anonymous, tough, humorous American in his long free verse tribute, *The People, Yes* (1936). Dos Passos for his part said "yes" to the native spirit in a historical portrait, *The Ground We Stand On* (1941).

The love-hate feeling for America was also evident in the work of John Steinbeck. Migrant workers and farmers pushed off their land were the heroes of such tender-brutal novels as *In Dubious Battle* (1936), *Of Mice and Men* (1937), and *The Grapes of Wrath* (1939)—the last two made into films which were even more moving than the books themselves. Steinbeck hated injustice. He hated to see waste, whether of human lives or of natural resources. He did not want American farmers to be peons or peasants. Yet, as with other commentators on the depression years, Steinbeck seemed also to dislike mass-production prosperity. He admired the poor, and at its best his sympathy was beautifully expressed. Was it possible also to admire those who were not poor? Here Steinbeck hesitated, and sometimes slipped into evasion and sentimentality.

James T. Farrell was a bleaker novelist, less caught up in hero-worship of the proletariat. The characters in his Chicago trilogy *Studs Lonigan* (1932–35) are not rich. But their poverty is spiritual rather than material. Young Lonigan and his friends are sullen and thwarted. They are in rebellion against the narrow righteousness of their

parents and of the Catholic church. But their own yearnings—for girls, popularity, money—are hardly less narrow. They grow stale and old all too quickly, like the food offered for sale in cheap neighborhood stores. Farrell's world is hemmed-in and grubby. His great virtue is honesty, and his readers in the 1930s praised him for refusing to succumb to proletarian myth, or to the somehow false exuberance of a writer like William Saroyan, who insisted that he loved everybody and that everybody was lovable.

Honesty of a different kind, and a more acceptable lyric quality than Saroyan's, was offered in the crowded autobiographical novels of Thomas Wolfe of North Carolina. During his short life—Wolfe died of pneumonia in 1938, at the age of thirty-seven—he wrote with prodigal energy, about himself, his home town, about the constant unavailing search of his fellow-Americans for a meaning in their existences. He was both a romantic and a realistic novelist. Where Farrell's prose was deliberately drab, Wolfe sought to embrace a whole continent with poetic fullness. Whether or not he was influenced by the poetry of Walt Whitman, Whitman was a part of the national heritage who meant a great deal to several writers of the 1930s. He too had loved his country as a vast collection of ordinary people. He too had despised those who went after false gods—fame, riches, gentility. The titles of Wolfe's novels—*Look Homeward, Angel* (1929), *Of Time and the River* (1935), *The Web and the Rock* (1939) and *You Can't Go Home Again* (1940)—indicate something of his vision of the restless quest for "the lost lane-end into heaven, a stone, a leaf, an unfound door. . . ."

In a way this was a nostalgic instinct, comparable with that of Rourke, Brooks, and Dos Passos. Wolfe was responding to the same combination of dismay at the present and pride in the past that sustained the program of southern intellectuals known as Agrarianism, or Lewis

Mumford's books on the rise of technology and the decline of cities as places it was possible to be happy in. Even before the onset of the depression the writer Sherwood Anderson had retired from the metropolis to live in a small Virginia town. The novelist Louis Bromfield, who had spent several years in France, retreated in 1939 to his home state Ohio to take up scientific farming.

At a popular level, several writers catered with great success to the general desire for escape routes out of the pressing reality of Great Depression America. Reading was itself a form of escape, and a fairly inexpensive one. With time on their hands, many people demanded long books in which they could lose themselves for days at a time. Historical novels, spiced with adventure, combat, romance, and sex, found a ready market. Hervey Allen's *Anthony Adverse* (1933), a lengthy tale of the Napoleonic Era, sold half a million copies in its first two years. Walter Edmonds did well with historical novels set in America, including *Drums Along the Mohawk* (1936). The

John Ford directed the compassionate movie of The Grapes of Wrath. *The double impact of best-selling book and film success spurred reform measures for California migrant workers.*

most spectacularly popular novel of the decade was *Gone With the Wind* (1936), by a Georgia lady named Margaret Mitchell who never wrote another book. Financially, she did not need to. *Gone With the Wind*, a story of Georgia during the Civil War and Reconstruction, had taken her ten years to finish. It was an immediate hit with the public, throughout the United States and indeed the whole world. At the height of its fame, 50,000 copies are said to have been sold in a single day. Later, as a film starring Clark Gable and Vivien Leigh, it enthralled fresh millions with its story of the loves and struggles of Scarlett O'Hara. For the readers of the 1930s, *Gone With the Wind* had everything. It could be relished for its sheer melodrama; bored housewives could imagine themselves gripped in the arms of the imperious Rhett Butler, and perhaps see their ineffectual husbands mirrored in the gentle failure, Ashley Wilkes. The novel could be interpreted as courage triumphing over poverty, or as the defeat of old values by commercialism. Above all, it was "unputdownably" readable.

If fiction hesitated between realism and romance, so did drama. The radical line was taken up in New York by the Theater Union and the Group Theater. Under their and other auspices Broadway was treated to some harsh exposés of social injustice. Some productions, such as Maxwell Anderson's *Winterset* (1935), a verse play based on the Sacco-Vanzetti case of the 1920s, were by established dramatists. Most of these showed a marked swing toward "Great Depression" themes, though Eugene O'Neill, the greatest figure in the American theater, wrote more or less as he had always done. The most striking new talent was that of Clifford Odets, a youngster who began working with the Group Theater. In 1935 two of his plays, the one-act *Waiting for Lefty* and *Awake and Sing*, were gripping New York. *Waiting for Lefty* could be labeled a propaganda play. The stage is supposed to be the platform of a labor union meeting, so that the audience serves as the mass of union members. A strike of taxi drivers is under discussion. Actors planted in the audience leap up to comment on the stage action. The play ends with the news that Lefty, the character for whom the meeting is waiting, has been killed. There is an immediate angry shout of "Strike! Strike!" The simplicity and ingenuity of Odets's staging achieved an extraordinary effect. *Awake and Sing* deals with a Jewish family in a Bronx tenement. The "awakening" is that of the son, Ralph Berger, who after trying to live for himself, at odds with his parents, decides that he must rise above the pettiness of domestic strife and commit himself as a revolutionist to the class struggle. Odets wrote some other powerful preachments before he was lured west to Hollywood.

Outside New York, the Federal Theater Project under the direction of Hallie Flanagan ran a nationwide program to find work for actors and stagehands. Traveling companies went all over the country, performing in schools, hospitals, camps and prisons, or in the open air, for an audience estimated at over 20 million people. Until the appropriation was cut off by a suspicious Congress in 1939, the Federal Theater was amazingly busy and resourceful. Among its successes were productions for black artists such as Orson Welles's *Macbeth*, and *The Hot Mikado*; a dramatization of Sinclair Lewis's antifascist novel *It Can't Happen Here* (with the idea that America *could* turn into a dictatorship); and "The Living Newspaper," a technique of presenting contemporary problems.

"The Living Newspaper" reminded Americans of the farmer's plight in *Triple-A Plowed Under*, and of the horrors of bad housing in *One-Third of a Nation*. They were similar in tone to the two haunting documentary films made by Pare Lorentz, *The Plow That Broke the Plains* (1936) and *The River* (1937), which presented the problems of soil erosion and flood control. At the other extreme were entertainments that aimed at nothing more than entertainment—girls, songs, comedy, glamor. In between came productions that tried to be amusing without being frivolous. Quite often they managed this unlikely feat. For instance, the stage version of Erskine Caldwell's salty story of southern sharecroppers, *Tobacco Road*, ran for over four years in New York. *Pins and Needles*, a revue mounted and performed by New York garment workers, was almost equally successful. Among its witty lyrics was one entitled "Sing Me a Song of Social Significance."

The Impact of Hollywood

Faulkner and Odets have been instanced as writers drawn to Hollywood. The novelist Scott Fitzgerald was a third. The movie capital sucked in talent from every field. Sam Goldwyn, for example, hired the dance director Busby Berkeley away from Broadway in 1930 to create extravaganzas like *Whoopee* and *Gold Diggers of 1933*. Faulkner was offered $500 a week for his first stint in Hollywood. Other celebrities were taken on the payroll for as much as $1,500 a week. Publicists for Hollywood could claim the motion picture industry was providing relief for American creative artists of all kinds on a bigger scale than the federal government. Critics argued that Hollywood was the kiss of death—a standardizer and ultimately a destroyer of individual talent.

Judged by the results, both arguments could be sustained. As in every other field, the movies sought to be both the conscience and the pacifier of the nation. At the beginning of the decade there was a vogue for "hard-hitting" gangster films; no less than fifty were churned out in a single year, 1931. The best, featuring gifted actors such as Edward G. Robinson and James Cagney, were excellent. *Little Caesar* (1930), *Public Enemy* (1931), and *Scarface* (1932) were fastmoving, violent and yet honest. But Hollywood's candor, also evident in early Mae West films, was a source of offense to censorship groups. Timid as always in face of such protest, Hollywood cleaned up its stories and dialogue. Instead of emphasizing the gangster, producers obliged J. Edgar Hoover by stressing the prowess of the FBI's "G-Men." Instead of sanctioning the adult portrayal of adult men and women, Hollywood went in for soft-focus glamor and merely hinted at scandal, or left that to the feline disclosures of gossip columnists Hedda Hopper and Louella Parsons. On screen, the stars were goddesses, elegantly gowned, impossibly

The flair and extravagant imagination of choreographer Busby Berkeley dazzled moviegoers in scenes like the ostrich feather fantasy in Fashions of 1934 (right). There were usually at least three spectacular set pieces in any musical he worked on, each costing about $10,000 a minute to produce. It was his elaborate sets, costuming, and groupings of girls in films like Dames (below), Ready Willing and Able (below right), and Gold Diggers of 1933 (far right) that won Berkeley fame.

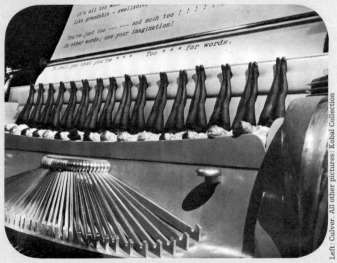

Gray depression days quickened the urge for entertainment and escape. Hollywood came to the rescue and, in the process, became the "film capital of the world." Left: Ginger Rogers and Fred Astaire, the most famous song-and-dance duo in movie history, in a typical shot from Shall We Dance? (1937). Right: James Cagney pushes a grapefruit into Mae Clarke's face in Public Enemy (1931). Below: Edward G. Robinson is shot by gangsters in Little Caesar (1930).

Kobal Collection

beautiful. The dream factory was in full swing, turning out Joan Crawfords, Carole Lombards, and Barbara Stanwycks in immaculate profusion.

Even so, many of these films of the 1930s still have plenty of life; not even Hollywood's primmest codes could disguise the appeal of the peroxide blonde Jean Harlow—in some respects an earlier version of Marilyn Monroe. They were synthetic, absurd, and yet electric. A Harlow or a Monroe in the role of good bad girl was a Hollywood stereotype. Perhaps, though, the stereotype corresponded to a genuine sort of American, hardboiled but wistful.

Late-night-TV addicts know that much of what Hollywood churned out in the 1930s was stock stuff. But a surprising amount reveals crisp dialogue and excellent acting—by small-part players as well as by the big stars: Greta Garbo, Katharine Hepburn, Myrna Loy, Charles Laughton, James Stewart. Each viewer will have his own favorites. Adding up the lists, one can see that Hollywood excelled in a number of distinct genres. Busby Berkeley musicals are still imitated by latter-day directors. Ken Russell's film of *The Boy Friend* (1972) is a case in point. Connoisseurs maintain that it is impossible to imitate the light skills of Fred Astaire and Ginger Rogers in dance films like *Roberta* (1935). Other movie buffs extol the sequence of Frank Capra social comedies (scripts by Robert Riskin) that began with Clark Gable and Claudette Colbert in *It Happened One Night* (1934), and continued with *Mr Deeds Goes To Town* (1936), *You Can't Take It With You* (1938), and *Mr Smith Goes To Washington* (1939). They were the sort of movies that the advertisements called "warm-hearted." The Great Depression was there in the background, but Capra told his audiences not to worry, not to complicate things. The simple old American virtues would win out. Small-town heroes, gangling and tongue-tied, would confront slick villainy and come off best. Sometimes they would back up their ideas with a phrase from Thomas Jefferson, or from Abe Lincoln—two of the decade's prime symbolic heroes.

Another Hollywood genre was the costume drama, based on a historical figure or a classic novel. These often began with titles in Gothic lettering on parchment sheets, or with a hand turning the pages of a supposedly ancient book. Sometimes they were heavyhanded; sometimes the cast looked out of place in period clothing. Often, however, they were excellent popularizations, as in *The Life of Emile Zola* (1937) and *Young Mr Lincoln* (1939). Of historical tales, *The Mutiny on the Bounty* (1935), based on Nordhoff and Hall's account of an actual episode in the British navy, amply justified its length and its expense. It immortalized Charles Laughton as the autocratic Captain Bligh, and added to Clark Gable's reputation with his portrayal of the mutineers' leader, Fletcher Christian.

As in the 1920s, though, Hollywood's best efforts were in comedy. Broadway's loss was their gain. Comic

performers from the stage were well equipped to act in front of the camera. Unlike Buster Keaton and some other stars of the silent days, they could easily make the transition to the "talkies." Eddie Cantor thrived as a singing comedian. Jimmy "Schnozzle" Durante traded on his big nose and his hoarse voice. W. C. Fields, occasionally paired with Mae West, kept alive the old spirit of vaudeville. Inspired casting gave him the role of Mr Micawber in *David Copperfield* (1935). Usually, however, he played himself—a crotchety old rascal in a straw hat, with a cigar stuck in the corner of his mouth, always on the lookout for a free drink and a soft touch. He usually wrote his own script, giving himself grotesque names like Otis J. Cribblecoblis. He delivered his lines out of the side of his mouth not occupied by the cigar, muttering insults, wisecracks, and lamentations. His comments were welcomely astringent after doses of Hollywood sugar. "No man who hates small dogs and children can be *all* bad" was a splendid line for audiences that had been watching little Shirley Temple deliver one of her

Above: Clark Gable and Vivien Leigh in Gone With the Wind *(1939). Its great acceptance proved the commercial viability of filming in color. Right: Comedians Oliver Hardy and Stan Laurel managed to bungle everything they attempted. Far right top: James Stewart and Jean Arthur in Frank Capra's social comedy,* Mr Smith Goes to Washington *(1939). Far right below: Riotous confusion dogged Harpo, Zeppo, Chico, and Groucho Marx in* A Night at the Opera *(1936).*

cute, precocious song-and-dance numbers. The viewers probably sensed that Fields meant what he said. Old professionals cannot afford to be generous to young ones.

The Marx Brothers—originally five, soon reduced to the famous trio of Groucho, Chico, and Harpo—also emerged from vaudeville. Groucho was the fast talker and aspiring con-man, with a moustache ludicrously painted on his upper lip, with a strange glide-crouch of a walk. Harpo was the gleeful clown who mimed instead of talking. Chico, a tiny hat perched on his curly head, was

the amiable go-between. Groucho's running fire of jokes no longer seems as funny as it once did. The interludes in which Chico plays the piano and Harpo plucks a harp have lost some of their magic. But when the Marx Brothers are in full swing, as in parts of *Duck Soup* (1933), *A Night at the Opera* (1936), and *A Day at the Races* (1937), there is a glorious swift lunacy, a richness of invention that has never been surpassed in the cinema. They had a good deal of competition, it must be admitted, from the team of Laurel and Hardy—two clumsy misfits, one thin and one fat, one nervous and melancholy, the other owlish and bullying. They had to compete also against the established genius of Charlie Chaplin. But unless we count *The Great Dictator* (1940), Chaplin made only two films in the 1930s, *City Lights* (1931) and *Modern Times* (1936). Each had its quota of Chaplinesque humor and pathos; Chaplin meant his audiences to laugh at some passages, and brush away a tear at others. They are extraordinary films, but the social message now appears a little elementary, the pathos a little manipulated.

Wooing the public was a serious business for Hollywood in the 1930s, especially in the early years of the Great Depression. Moviegoing had dropped off alarmingly. Audiences had to be won back, primarily by making films that people wanted to see but also by other devices. One idea, invented by the manager of a movie theater in Colorado, was "Bank Night"—an evening each week in which prizes were offered. Another notion, introduced partly to give customers their money's worth and partly to enforce distribution of lesser films, was the double feature. In other words, the coupling of two pictures, an "A" and a "B." In between them was wedged a newsreel and a cartoon, with possibly a Wurlitzer organ interlude.

The newsreel format was greatly extended in 1935 by the "March of Time" series. These, an offshoot of *Time*

Moviemaker Walt Disney created an animated world with a variety of lovable creatures. Mickey Mouse, his 1929 brainchild, helps Disney inspect some film (left). Snow White examines Doc, Sleepy, Happy, Sneezy, Bashful, Grumpy, and Dopey for clean hands before dinner in Snow White and the Seven Dwarfs (below). The Three Little Pigs make music for the Silly Symphony (right).

magazine, were documentary films on particular subjects. Each was a compact, well edited, dramatically narrated film essay, ending with the signature phrase "TIME—MARCHES—ON!" As for cartoons, these too were transformed by the efforts of Walt Disney. Disney carried off the motion picture Academy Award for cartoons in every year of the 1930s. His first creation was Mickey Mouse, in black and white. He added other characters, notably Donald Duck and Goofy the dog, who superseded Mickey and Minnie. He introduced color cartoons. In 1933 Disney captivated audiences with his *Three Little Pigs*—this the cartoon that launched the song-hit "Who's Afraid of the Big Bad Wolf?" His 1934 Academy Award was for his version of *The Tortoise and the Hare*. Subsequent winning nominations included *The Old Mill* and *Ferdinand the Bull*. His boldest venture in 1938 was the full length *Snow White and the Seven Dwarfs*. *Snow White* packed the cinemas at a time when, because of a fresh recession, attendance was down by as much as 40 per cent. Its popularity was challenged by the film of *Gone With the Wind*, a mammoth production, and to a lesser extent by *Goodbye, Mr Chips* and *Stagecoach*. *Snow White* had the advantage, though, of spinoff in other markets. Its songs—"Heigh-ho, Heigh-ho," "Whistle While You Work," "Some Day My Prince Will Come"—became hits. The toy industry, otherwise short of work, went into crash production to manufacture rubber models of Snow White, Grumpy, Dopey, and the other dwarfs.

In addition to such Disney ditties, the public had a rich choice in other music. This was the era of the crooner, and supremely of Bing Crosby—known as yet mainly through records and radio. The "hot jazz" of the 1920s was somewhat out of fashion during the years of the first Roosevelt administration. The public on the whole preferred sweet music with a slow tempo. "Star Dust," "Night and Day," and "Stormy Weather" were immensely popular. This sort of song held its own. But gradually enthusiasm grew for quicker, noisier work. "The Music Goes Round and Around" was a brief craze of the mid-1930s. Then came the period of the big bands—Louis Armstrong, Count Basie, Artie Shaw, Duke Ellington, Tommy Dorsey, Benny Goodman—and the day of swing. The clarinetist Benny Goodman was known as the King of Swing. By 1938 swing had thousands of young devotees, and a whole vocabulary of its own. Swing "sent" its admirers. A "jam session" put them "in the groove." The "alligators" would leap up when they heard the "boogie-woogie" beat and begin to "jitterbug."

Moralists were horrified, as they had been over the advent of jazz twenty years earlier—or indeed as they had been long before when the waltz came into fashion. But there was music to suit all tastes. The 1930s also witnessed a revival of folksong. There was the semi-highbrow music of George Gershwin, seductively attractive in the folk opera *Porgie and Bess* (1935). There was a medley of compositions from Aaron Copland, including *Billy the Kid* (1938), based on cowboy songs. Along with much "schmaltz" radio provided abundant offerings of orchestral and chamber music.

In fact radio could be regarded as the central medium of the era. Television barely existed. Radio filled the airwaves. Those who had hoped for a controlled development, keeping commercialism to a minimum, deplored the failure of the federal government to issue licences according to a proper code. Instead, local stations came on the air by the hundred. The discovery of FM (frequency modulation) increased the spread of available wavelengths. The result was a crazy quilt of programs, mostly dominated by the advertisers who paid for them. The new medium had insatiable demands. Its hourage had to be filled—and was filled with a mélange of commercial plugs and jingles, sandwiched between talk and quiz shows, disk-jockey hours, news flashes, soap operas, and the like. Pessimists might well talk of pollution of the airwaves, and express alarm that demagogues like Father Coughlin, or dubious gospelers and quack medicine men, could buy their own programs, even their own stations.

In retrospect the worst fears seem vastly exaggerated. Some stations such as WQXR in New York concentrated on "good" music. NBC had a prodigious success with weekend broadcasts of opera and symphony music. In

Brown Brothers

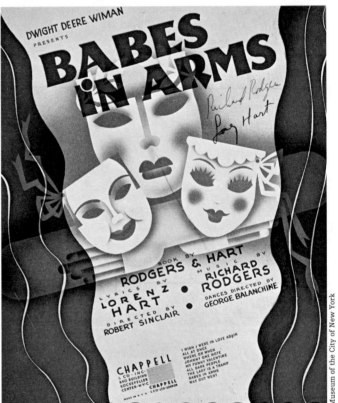

Museum of the City of New York

Jazz rhythms surfaced in the popular music of the 1930s as "swing." Richard Rodgers and Lorenz Hart had a Broadway success with "Babes in Arms." Bandleaders like Count Basie (top) dominated the big bands touring the country. The legendary Benny Goodman and his sextet (top right) dazzled admirers with their smooth musicianship and set them jitterbugging (right) in their smart new saddle shoes.

Top: Brown Brothers. Bottom, both pictures: UPI

fact, radio actually stimulated interest in music. The number and quality of symphony orchestras grew steadily. Whether radio diminished the habit of reading was debatable. Those who thought it did pointed out that the average household listened to radio for between four and five hours a day. How could those hours be used for reading? Yet the better programs, among which were Clifton Fadiman's "Information Please," "Invitation to Learning," and "Town Meeting of the Air," were wholesomely educational. Of many commentators, Raymond Gram Swing, H. V. Kaltenborn, and Lowell Thomas gained a national following. Among their juniors were broadcasters of the caliber of Edward R. Murrow.

The situation of newspapers was analogous: masses of advertising, a lot of trivial items, and islands of excellence. The newspaper equivalent of a Kaltenborn was the syndicated columnist. Readers could take their choice between, say, the breathless gossip of Walter Winchell (who was also a regular broadcaster), or Eleanor Roosevelt's good-natured column "My Day." They could enjoy the ferocity of Westbrook Pegler, who hated the New Deal and said so; they could appreciate the more dignified analyses of Walter Lippmann, who likewise made known his doubts about the Roosevelt policies. They could weigh the words of Dorothy Thompson, an influential columnist who was married to the novelist Sinclair Lewis, or glean the inside story on some political tangle from Drew Pearson. No matter how serious their concern for news and interpretation, sober readers were no different from other Americans in turning to the comics page to follow the latest bulletin on the adventures of Tarzan, Superman, or Little Orphan Annie. In radio the equivalents were comedians such as Jack Benny, or Burns and Allen; the back-chat of Edgar Bergan, the ventriloquist with his unnervingly intelligent dummy Charlie McCarthy; and the serial dramas. Of these one of the most eagerly listened to was "The Lone Ranger," which started in 1933 and by 1939 was heard thrice weekly by some 20 million people.

The most addictive of all was "Amos 'n' Andy," a carry-over from the 1920s. Amos and his friend Andy were supposed to be two Negroes involved in running the Fresh Air Taxicab Company, Incorpulated. With them were associated Madame Queen, Ruby, the Kingfish, and so on. All the male parts were played by two white actors, Freeman F. Gosden and Charles J. Correll. The program started with WMAQ in Chicago, then moved to NBC in New York. It had to be broadcast twice each evening, at 7 PM for easterners and at 11:30 PM for listeners west of the Mississippi. It was like a fifteen-minute serial strip cartoon, avidly awaited all over the Union. Amos was hardworking and sensible, Andy the self-proclaimed mastermind, always "layin' down to think." Were they racial stereotypes? Black Americans said so in the 1960s, when an abortive attempt was made to revive the program. Within the climate of opinion of the 1930s, the

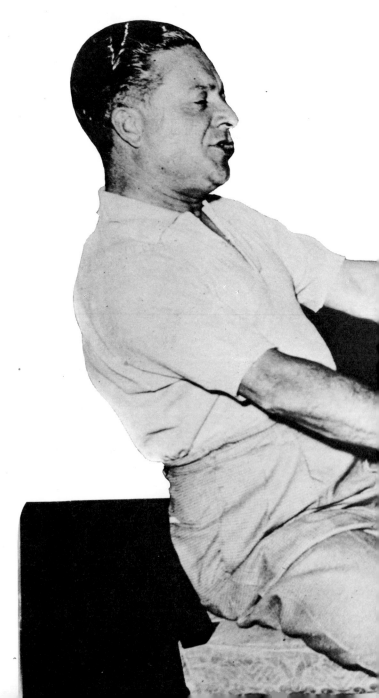

Families gathered around the radio for the easy laughter of Fibber McGee and Molly (above) or Burns and Allen (top right). Even ventriloquism was made to work over the airwaves; Edgar Bergen and his too-intelligent dummy, Charlie McCarthy (top left) were widely popular. But Freeman Gosden and Charles Correll's Amos 'n' Andy (below) reached the widest and most devoted audience of all.

"The Martians have landed!"

At eight o'clock on the evening of October 30, 1938, America was tuning in to The Mercury Theater of the Air, directed by and starring Orson Welles, already known as an innovator on the American stage at only twenty-three. That Sunday his brilliant adaptation of H. G. Wells's *The War of the Worlds* caused panic and hysteria among hundreds of thousands of listeners.

After the customary station identification and introduction by Welles, both of which made it clear that a studio drama was to follow, a series of "news flashes" told the old story of a Martian "invasion." The original tale was updated to the present and the setting was changed to a real village in New Jersey. Millions just tuning in their radios heard a weather report and then dance music from a fictitious hotel. Suddenly, a bulletin interrupted to the effect that astronomers had observed large explosions on Mars. This was followed by more announcements from Intercontinental Radio News (also fictitious). A "meteor" had landed in New Jersey killing 1,500. The story picked up at ludicrous speed. It was not a meteor but a "metal cylinder" and the militia was called out and now something horrible came out "wriggling like a great snake . . . as large as a bear and it glitters like wet leather. . . . The eyes are black and gleam like serpents. The mouth is U-shaped with saliva dripping from rimless lips that seem to quiver and pulsate. . . . What's that? There's a jet of flame . . . and it leaps right at the advancing men. Good Lord! They're turning into flame! . . . It's coming this way. . . ."

And so on: poisonous black smoke and death rays, the destruction of New Jersey and the evacuation of New York City. . . . It was a Sunday broadcast, and three times after the introduction the announcer had explained that it was just a dramatization. But Americans listened and believed—and panicked.

Weeping and hysterical women swamped the switchboards of the *Providence Journal* for details of the "massacre and destruction." Five Princeton University geologists rushed off to the scene of the "landing" to examine the "cylinder." In San Francisco, the impression was widespread that the Eastern Seaboard had been overrun by invaders who were in the process of heading west. Mass hysteria was so high that many people telephoned police and news services to claim that they had witnessed the "invasion." At least one police station advised inquirers to follow the advice on their radios.

It only lasted an hour, but the effect of the program, which had been entirely unforeseen, was not easily dismissed. Orson Welles, unshaven and sleepless, apologized the next afternoon at CBS studios. The government instituted an investigation that eventually absolved both Welles and CBS of any wrongdoing (but no radio station since has dared use the same format to dramatize false events).

Perhaps some of the reaction can be explained by the nervousness of a public which had listened to similar broadcasts only a month earlier reporting Chamberlain's capitulation at Munich. What the incident had done most clearly was demonstrate the authority of the new medium. People, like a woman who disrupted an Indianapolis church service during the broadcast, hardly bothered to question the authoritative voice that came into their living-rooms. This particular woman had run into the service screaming, "It's the end of the world! You might as well go home to die. I just heard it on the radio." And they went home.

Twenty-three-year-old Orson Welles terrorized America with his production of "The War of the Worlds" in 1938.

Culver Pictures

series was innocent enough. The appeal lay in the universality. Americans black or white laughed *with* Amos and Andy rather than *at* them. The dialogue, with catch phrases like "Check and double check" and "I'ze regusted" (disgusted), was possibly condescending. But according to one "Amos 'n' Andy" fan, the basic theme was "the perennial fight of some one to keep his money from getting into the hands of some one else who is trying to get it away from him. This is the drama in which we are all engaged. . . . Each evening money is in the background. The Kingfish is trying to get Amos's $100, to give some of it to the Battleaxe, and Amos, with his honest simplicity, yet shrewd mind, is determined that the Battleaxe shall have none of it. America is interested in that conflict."

The media were all fighting for the public's allegiance. The amount of spare cash was limited. The question was whether people could afford to buy newspapers *and* radios, novels *and* phonograph records, theater or movie tickets *and* magazine subscriptions. On the whole the answer was yes, though baseball and football receipts fell off in the Great Depression. One reason was that the media's services did not cost much, even on limited budgets. A second reason was that people craved news, guidance, and entertainment. America was bewildered, anxious. The depression was, in a word, depressing. Anyone who could supply a tonic, whether in laughter, tunefulness, or clear analysis, was in demand. Studs Terkel's book of interviews, *Hard Times* (1970), brings this out in fascinating personal terms. Looking back on the depression, most of the people he talked to confessed they had been worried, broke, and often ashamed. Others, in the entertainment business, tended to admit that they had thrived, because America craved their wares.

This is clearly illustrated in the magazine field. *Time,* the *New Yorker,* the *Saturday Evening Post* and other periodicals continued to increase their sales. Most of the new ventures similarly succeeded in carving out a sizable readership, even when as with *Fortune* (1930) and *Esquire* (1933) they were quite expensive. These two magazines offered a sort of low-cost opulence. *Fortune* reassured the businessman that his realm was still important: there were still fortunes to be made. *Esquire* discovered a market, later to be exploited by *Playboy,* for spicy sophistication. *Newsweek* (1933) competed with *Time* for readers who demanded a lively, compact guide to current affairs. In 1936 Henry Luce, the proprietor of *Time* and *Fortune,* added the weekly picture magazine *Life* to his empire. This, too, soon captured a wide audience, ready to agree with Luce that a good photograph needed only a brief caption to convey a story that might have required a thousand words to get across. As a humorist was later to remark, the American public began to consist of *Post*men, *Fortune*hunters, *Time*servers and *Life*buoys. He could have added "*Digest*ives," for *Reader's Digest* counted its audience in the millions,

even if another periodical, the old *Literary Digest,* went out of business in 1938. The usual explanation is that the *Literary Digest,* which had been conducting straw polls in advance of presidential elections, was disastrously wrong in 1936, a landslide year for Roosevelt. The *Digest's* poll predicted a landslide victory for FDR's opponent, Governor Alfred Landon. In the subsequent ridicule the *Digest* lost the confidence of its readers. Another explanation may be that public tastes shifted, sometimes quickly and inexplicably. Americans seemed to insist upon a formula, a familiar format. Then suddenly they would grow tired of sameness and look for novelty.

So the United States moved through the depression years, in need simultaneously of amusement and instruction. On the whole the nation was well served by its spokesmen and entrepreneurs, no matter how contradictory the pull between anger and escape, art and kitsch. Writers and artists and painters and moviemakers and songsters provided the symbols, the words, the tunes that people need in any era to define their identities. In the Great Depression this need was doubly great, because Americans did not know whether to take an entirely new road, or merely to repair the old one. One final example of their doubleness lies in architecture. There was less money for ambitious building projects than in the 1920s. But out of economy in resources architects fashioned a theory of functionalism. Ornament, they said, was unnecessary, even dishonest. A building ought to be defined by its purpose and its basic structure. Clean, bare surfaces, windows, light, lightness were the new idiom, exemplified by the buildings of Walter Gropius and Frank Lloyd Wright. If the engineer acquired a new prominence, so much the better. The Rockefeller Center in New York was a monument to technology (as well as something of an exhibition space for sculptors and muralists), a soaring, planned complex, a statement of confidence in the future. So was the Boulder Dam (later renamed the Hoover Dam). So were the TVA dams in the Tennessee Valley. So, gloriously, was the George Washington Bridge across the Hudson River, and the Golden Gate Bridge in the San Francisco bay. They seemed truly heroic—declarations of courage, craft, and community. More selfconsciously and less convincingly, there were also the two big expositions, Chicago's Century of Progress and New York's World of Tomorrow. These were not landmarks in the history of architecture. Even so, they brought a breath of brash optimism for millions.

Art, anger, escape. In essence, the message conveyed to America, whether in banal and sentimental or in grimly searching ways, was that good could come from bad. Hard times could lead to a rethinking, perhaps a reaffirmation of what America stood for—or would no longer stand for. Sincerity conceded that the wolf was at the door. Hope enjoined the belief that the wolf could be kept outside, and driven away.

Angelo Hornak

Angelo Hornak. Below : Elliot Erwitt/Magnum

Angelo Hornak

Angelo Hornak

By Courtesy of the Victoria and Albert Museum

In 1936 Frank Lloyd Wright cantilevered "Falling Water" (left) over a stream in Pennsylvania. It was designed as a residence for Edgar J. Kaufmann, a Pittsburgh businessman whose office, also designed by Wright, is shown above. Surprisingly, the architect was denied any part in the design of New York's Rockefeller Center, also built in the 1930s. Top, right to left: The Center's RCA Building, a doorway decorated with Steuben glass, Ladies Powder Room by Yasuo Kunyoshi, and Roxy's Private Suite by Donald Deskey.

Chapter 5

Making Recovery Work

The New Deal encouraged the growth of organized labor and involved a determined attempt to lift farm incomes. Although some gains had been made earlier, only the New Deal fostered the right of American workingmen to organize and bargain collectively. Encouraged by this, the CIO was formed. It brought millions of factory workers under the umbrella of unionism. Hostile employers often opposed labor's new rights, and violence erupted in cities and towns. Violence also surfaced in the angry countryside. Farmers, who had failed to share in the prosperity of the 1920s, were badly hurt by overproduction, falling prices, and indebtedness. The New Deal's agriculture policies did not always succeed, but they did help make farming profitable again.

The Right to Organize

During the Great Depression, the majority of Americans came to recognize the right of workers to organize labor unions. As part of the New Deal, Congress passed legislation designed to assist the growth of the labor movement. With this encouragement, labor union membership tripled to over 10 million.

Events in the 1920s paved the way for the expansion of organized labor. As secretary of commerce and then president, Herbert Hoover sought to end the class conflict which had erupted during the Red Scare of 1919. He believed that prosperity and voluntary negotiation, rather than government interference, would cure the labor ills of the nation. He rejoiced that by the mid-1920s, "owing to public opinion and some pushing on our part, the twelve-hour day was on the way out in American industry." Hoover was glad this advance for labor had been achieved "without the aid of a single law."

There were signs in the 1920s that the courts were going to give labor a fair deal. For example, in the railroad industry it came to be recognized that an employer-sponsored "company union" was not an acceptable legal substitute for a worker-dominated labor union. In 1926, Hoover helped to arrange conferences between bosses and unions leading to the Railway Labor Act of that year which banned company unions in the railroad industry. The Texas and New Orleans Railroad, which nurtured such a union, tested the constitutionality of the law. In 1930, just after Hoover's appointment of Charles Evans Hughes as chief justice, the Supreme Court adjudicated in *Texas and New Orleans Railroad Co* v *Brotherhood of Railway and Steamship Clerks*. When the 1926 act was upheld, labor unionists were delighted, although they regretted that it applied only to the railroad industry.

Labor hailed the Norris-LaGuardia Act of 1932 as a further gain. The Democrats who pushed it through Congress hoped that it would abolish labor injunctions. Judges had for decades issued injunctions prohibiting union coercion during strikes. Such injunctions implied that coercion was in fact taking place, whereas very often there had only been an allegation of intimidation, filed by an employer. The practical value of the 1932 act is uncertain. Yet it did remove a device whereby union men could be arbitrarily designated criminals. For union members, the Republican years (1920–33) obviously had redeeming features, even if they ended in economic disaster.

In 1928 John L. Lewis, president of the United Mine Workers of America, described Hoover as the country's "foremost industrial statesman." Eight years later a mineworker warmly declared: "Mr Roosevelt is the only man we ever had in the White House who would understand that my boss is a sonofabitch." Roosevelt provoked the warmer response among workingmen because his party was more willing to legislate on their behalf.

The National Industrial Recovery Act, passed soon after Roosevelt's inauguration in 1933, established the National Recovery Administration (NRA) and extended the provisions of the 1926 Railway Labor Act to the whole of the work force. The American Federation of Labor, which like Hoover opposed government intervention in the labor market, frustrated attempts to include general minimum wage requirements in the 1933 act, but these could be negotiated industry by industry under the protection of NRA "codes" of fair business practice. Section 7(a) of the Recovery Act confirmed that workingmen had the "right to organize and bargain collectively through representatives of their own choosing." This section was soon given teeth. Senator Robert F. Wagner of New York became chairman of a National Labor Board, with power to supervise and legitimize elections among employees seeking to authenticate the representative character of their labor organizations. In theory, employers would now have to recognize and deal with democratically constituted labor unions.

When the Supreme Court invalidated the NRA codes in 1935, it became necessary to find a substitute for Section 7(a). The Court's decision gave new urgency to thoroughgoing labor reforms which Wagner had been steering through Congress. Within six weeks of that decision, FDR had added his presidential signature to the National Labor Relations Act, more commonly known as the Wagner Act. The Wagner Act reaffirmed Section 7(a) and supplied permanent machinery for its enforcement. A three-man National Labor Relations Board was to supervise union elections and ensure that employers refrained from "unfair labor practices." Unfair practices were defined to include not only refusal to bargain, but also the turning down of "closed shop" agreements whereby employees would be forced to join a union. In 1937, the radical Wagner Act went into full effect when the Supreme Court passed favorably upon it. Organized labor could but applaud the legislative achievements of the Roosevelt government.

Federal administrators induced employers to subscribe to NRA codes by granting them immunity from antitrust prosecution. For example, according to Code of Fair Competition No. 1, administered by the Cotton Textile National Industrial Relations Board, cotton producers in 1933 accepted Section 7(a), and in return were allowed to restrict production in order to push up prices. However, employers were not obliged to negotiate NRA codes, and many held out against them. Workers whose hopes had been raised by the new laws often found that they had to fight for the "right to organize."

Section 7(a) stirred interest in unionism in Minneapolis, and led to a chaotic strike involving Local 574 of the International Brotherhood of Teamsters. Minneapolis,

although still the distributive center of the Northwest, was by 1934 a city in economic decline. For a 54 to 90 hour week, its teamsters received a mere $12 to $18, and were sometimes paid off in bruised vegetables. The Citizens' Alliance, an antiunion employers' association, refused to deal with Local 574 when its left-wing leadership presented demands in conformity with the rules laid down in Section 7(a). Dan Tobin, the standpat national president of the teamsters, denounced Local 574 for its communistic tendencies. It was only after the death of

Armed with new legislative support, the unions were active, organizing workers and demanding better pay and conditions. Joe Jones captured the sense of urgency generated by the depression in We Demand *(left). After violence erupted during the San Francisco general strike in 1934, Martin Fletcher painted a striker and strikebreaker fighting on the docks in* Trouble in Frisco *(above).*

four men in street fighting, the imposition of martial law by Governor Floyd B. Olson, and the personal intervention of FDR that the capitalists and workers of Minneapolis came to terms in the spirit of Section 7(a).

In 1934, employers' intransigence and industrial strife were by no means confined to Minneapolis. The San Francisco general strike of July pivoted on the longshoremen's dispute with the Industrial Association, the city's equivalent of the Minneapolis Citizens' Alliance. The equivalent of Tobin in the San Francisco strike was Joseph P. Ryan, president of the International Longshoremen's Association, a corrupt and self-indulgent official once heard to remark: "Next to myself, I like silk underwear best." Ryan was unable to restrain dockers who, incensed at the local company union and disgusted with

the arbitrary hiring system known as the "shape-up," responded to the communistic leadership of an Australian immigrant, Harry Bridges. Because of the violent clashes which took place between union pickets and strikebreakers, San Francisco employers appealed to Roosevelt to break the strike. Roosevelt, then cruising in the Pacific aboard the USS *Houston*, chose restraint, and the West Coast longshoremen won a satisfactory settlement of their grievances.

The industrial troubles of 1934 assumed the proportions of an epidemic when, in a massive Labor Day stoppage, textile workers struck in twenty states. State governors and local sheriffs took firm repressive measures. In one incident in South Carolina, where pay and working conditions were particularly miserable, six union pickets were shot dead. The tragedy of the textile war was that, while the industry paid lip service to Section 7(a), the Cotton Textile National Industrial Relations Board failed to implement federal policy.

One of the lessons of 1934 was that, while legislation might provide labor unions with an opportunity for expansion, good organization was still needed. Another lesson was that the AFL was incapable of providing it. Some leaders of AFL unions, for example David Dubinsky of the garment workers, still possessed the necessary vigor. But there were too many like Tobin and Ryan who were inert, corrupt, or both. AFL leaders continued to defend, as they had always done, the principles of craft unionism. Mostly of northwest European stock themselves, they were contemptuous of the semiskilled immigrant masses from southern and eastern Europe— "rubbish," Tobin called them—who worked in factories. When they did attempt to organize factory workers, they tried to fit them into a variety of craft unions instead of into one "industrial" union. Factory wage earners could see no sense in this. Of the 100,000 steelworkers who responded enthusiastically to an organizing drive in 1933, only 6,000 remained organized by the following year because of the AFL methods.

Birth of the CIO

A new initiative was needed in 1934, and John L. Lewis of the mineworkers provided it. Lewis perceived, even before Section 7(a) was on the statute books, that labor would have to fight hard to avail itself of the coming opportunity. He went to work on the AFL leadership, offering half a million dollars from the mineworkers' own funds toward an organizing drive among factory workers. At the AFL convention of 1934, he thought he had secured agreement in principle on the necessity for an organizing drive on industrial lines, only to discover over the next year that he had been "beguiled" and "seduced with fair words." In the 1935 convention, the enraged and frustrated Lewis went so far as to punch one of his conservative opponents, "Big Bill" Hutcheson of the Carpenters' Union. The blow symbolized the split between industrial and craft unionists, for Lewis, with the assistance of Sidney Hillman of the garment workers, formed a defiant Committee for Industrial Organization. Expelled from the AFL in 1936, the committee became the Congress of Industrial Organizations. The breakaway industrial unionists launched a massive organizing campaign among factory workers. By 1941, the CIO had, with astonishing rapidity, recruited a membership of 2.6 million. Such was the appeal of the CIO that most people believed its inflated claim to have 5 million members, as many as the AFL.

The reputation of the CIO was partly founded on the bombast of John L. Lewis. Lewis mesmerized America. His 230-pound frame frequently and effectively quivered to the resonance of a thunderous oratory. Ethnically acceptable to conservatives by virtue of his Welsh descent, "John L." was the constant target of bribes and enticements. But, remaining true to the miners and to the labor movement, Lewis resisted every blandishment, even the invitation to become secretary of labor in the Coolidge cabinet. His objective was independent power, both for himself and for organized labor. This led him to insulate himself from criticism within the miners' union by appointing sycophants and family members to subordinate administrative positions. It was fortunate for the CIO that Lewis was complemented within that organization by the powerful figure of Sidney Hillman.

A Lithuanian Jew, Hillman reflected the "new" immigrant composition of his union, the Amalgamated Clothing Workers of America. He symbolized the support of immigrant factory labor for the CIO. In addition to revitalizing unionism in the needle trades, he succeeded in unionizing half the textile workers in America through the CIO's Textile Workers' Organizing Committee. When Lewis quarreled with Roosevelt after supporting his reelection in 1936, Hillman became labor's leading mouthpiece in Washington. Perhaps because he had been a Socialist in his youth, Hillman forged the strongest possible links between government and labor. No revolutionary, however, he spoke for a majority within the CIO in warning "we cannot wreck the house in which we expect to live."

House-wrecking appeared to be the prerogative of employers, not unions, in 1937. This was the verdict of even conservative newspapers when the "Little Steel" dispute shattered the domestic tranquility of the nation. In May of 1937, after the CIO's Steel Workers' Organizing Committee had recruited 300,000 members, the traditionally antiunion United States Steel Corporation came to terms with Lewis. "Little Steel"—a group of smaller companies whipped into battle fury by industrialist Tom

The CIO's efforts to unionize steel workers led to the "Little Steel" dispute of 1937. Workers struck and marched in protest (right) against the antiunion policies of some smaller steel companies which then brought in armed strike breakers. Below: A worker is clubbed in Cleveland. Below right: Shotgun-bearing "goons" meet pickets at Auxbridge, Pennsylvania.

Girdler—successfully held out against the CIO. "Little Steel" won, however, by using heavily armed private armies known as "goon squads" to disperse and intimidate union pickets.

Lewis passed judgment. Girdler, he announced, was "a heavily armed monomaniac, with murderous tendencies, who has gone berserk." Events in the automobile industry reinforced this image of the American capitalist. In 1937, the CIO-inspired United Automobile Workers confronted first General Motors and then Chrysler with "sit-down" tactics, whereby strikers occupied their factories and stopped production. Eventually unions admitted that sit-downs were illegal, and stopped using them. By this time, they had extracted agreements from the auto industry. During the period of confrontation, however, it emerged that auto manufacturers employed goon squads and, in addition, a host of paid informers or "company spies." Most of the spies were out to feather their own nests by exploiting both

sides in an industrial dispute. This did not prevent workers from becoming extremely indignant at the ostensible role of the spy, which was to demoralize unions from within and warn employers of impending trouble. A Congressional Committee on Civil Liberties under the chairmanship of Senator Robert La Follette, Jr created widespread public concern over employers' tactics by exposing the degree to which big corporations financed goon squads and espionage.

The popular outcry against employers' tactics, together with widespread criticism of their refusal to comply with Section 7(a) and the Wagner Act, encouraged the great upward surge in union membership between 1933 and 1937. Pro-labor public opinion discouraged elected officials from breaking strikes by force, and helped to guarantee the right to organize where New Deal legislation sometimes failed. On the other hand, it was by identifying closely with the middle-of-the-road politics of the New Deal that the CIO continued to inspire confidence. Lewis acted to save the labor movement both from the right-wing extreme of company unionism, and from the left-wing extreme of communism. Accused of playing along with the Communists, Lewis arrogantly invoked the distinction between retriever dogs (the Communists) and the hunter (Lewis)—who gets the bird?

The rise in union membership in the 1930s is attributable to the adaptability of the CIO to the moderate New Deal outlook, and to the consequent acceptance of unionism by the American public. Previous labor advances, for example in the early 1830s and late 1890s, had occurred in similar circumstances. Another factor to be considered in relation to union growth is the persistence of unemployment in the 1930s. There were still 9 million out of work in 1939. Workers were goaded by a sense of grievance into organizing. Earlier depressions, such as those of 1873–78 and 1893–97, had been periods of declining membership. But in those years workingmen, though rebellious in outlook, lacked the encouragement of a liberal public and helpful government. Such encouragement was present in abundance at the height of the New Deal.

A Shift in Public Attitudes

Always fickle, public support ebbed away from the union movement after 1937. A stagnation in membership growth set in. People were less enthusiastic about union power in the later 1930s not because of any sudden accretion in sympathy for the employers, but because of a growing distrust of labor. Unions were a burgeoning political force, and rumors flew concerning the size and effect of "slush funds" in the hands of top officials at election time. Strikers were increasingly regarded as a

selfish group out to improve their own lot at the expense of their fellow workers. Above all, union power was resented and attacked when it seemed to undermine public morality and liberal ideology. The issues of corruption and communism alienated support not only from the labor movement, but from its mainstay, the New Deal.

Perhaps because they had outgrown the youthful idealism of the nineteenth century, the older AFL unions were more vulnerable to corruption than the CIO. The repeal of prohibition encouraged the Capone mob to look for new sources of revenue, and they muscled in on the bartenders' union within the Chicago Loop. In New York, Dutch Schultz milked the restaurant industry through the unions. His bogus Metropolitan Association "protected" employers against bogus strikes. Thomas E. Dewey, a special prosecutor appointed to investigate racketeering, described Schultz's association as "a $2 million shakedown." In spite of the urgent prompting of internal reformers like Dubinsky, the AFL failed to get rid of its racketeers. The voting public made their feelings known when, in 1938, Dewey only narrowly missed being

elected governor of New York State.

In contrast to the AFL, the youthful and radical CIO attracted the support of a number of Communists. Witnesses before the House Committee on Un-American Activities, established in 1938 under the chairmanship of Representative Martin Dies of Texas, identified Communist leanings in 280 unions. On one level, these accusations were ridiculous—the Boy Scouts and Camp Fire Girls were also under suspicion. But smear tactics could be politically effective. Governor Frank Murphy of Michigan had refused to use troops to dislodge sit-down strikers at Flint. For this he incurred right-wing wrath, and was dubbed a Communist-CIO pawn before the Dies committee. As a result of such propaganda, and of a changing political climate, he lost the gubernatorial contest of 1938.

FDR had always been impatient with the minutiae of collective bargaining legislation, and the antiunion shift in public opinion gave him political justification for a change in emphasis. He called for legislation to help all workers, not just the privileged few organized into labor unions. The 1935 Social Security Act had established a national system of old age and unemployment insurance, and had extended federal aid to public health services in the states. The Fair Labor Standards Act of 1938 put on a permanent basis those NRA codes which had regulated child labor, and established a forty-cent-per-hour minimum wage and forty-hour maximum work week in American industry.

The acts of 1935 and 1938 contained many loopholes and exemptions designed to accommodate the objections of constitutional lawyers and of interest group lobbyists. Some of the most needy, such as farmworkers, failed to benefit. Dies filed a satirical amendment to the 1938 proposal: "Within 90 days after the appointment of the Administrator, she shall report to Congress whether anyone is subject to this bill." But in the eyes of social reformers who had viewed with alarm the effects of union growth and power, the Fair Labor Standards Act was the best as well as the last of the great New Deal measures. In their view, the welfare state was more important than the right to organize.

The CIO's attempts to unionize the automobile industry met with concerted obstruction and flat rejection by the industry's leaders. Workers at the General Motors plant in Flint, Michigan, replied by declaring a sit-down strike in January, 1937.

The Farmer's Plight

The crisis facing the farmers in 1932 stemmed in large part from conditions that had been aggravating them since the First World War. The war years and the brief interlude following, had brought a prosperity farmers had not known for years. They bought expensive land, machinery, animals, fertilizers, automobiles, and personal luxuries, borrowing money to pay for them in the belief that good times had come to stay.

Unfortunately, the anticipated endless prosperity came to a sudden end in the early 1920s. European nations resumed peacetime production and encouraged their farmers to produce, hoping to become more self-sufficient in food and raw materials. Much of the foreign market, as a consequence, began vanishing for the American farmer who also had to contend with falling prices and the growing competition of Canada, Australia, and Argentina. The emergence of the United States from the war as a creditor nation did not help matters, either. The shortage of real currency in Europe made it difficult to dispose of the usual quantities of American products. Competition stiffened and conditions were worsened by the adoption of marketing quotas, exchange controls, tariff restrictions, and import and export licenses that further impeded international trade.

At home a dwindling market, accumulating surpluses, falling prices, crushing debts, and the advance of technology posed other serious problems. The ability to consume food simply could not keep pace with production. The use of more trucks, tractors, and automobiles meant that fewer horses and mules were used on the farm, and about 35 million acres formerly used to produce feed crops for farm animals were now available for other needs. The release of these 35 million acres and the accessibility of another 40 million acres brought into cultivation during the war years meant that an additional 75 million acres became available to raise food for human consumption. Greater efficiency on the farm also aggravated matters. Production per farm worker had increased about 21 per cent between 1909 and 1919 and it grew even more during the 1920s. Farming, as a result, became less important as a source of income. In the boom years of 1918–19 agriculture accounted for 25 per cent of the total income; but by 1929 it accounted for only slightly more than 10 per cent and in 1933 for slightly less than 9 per cent.

Republican efforts to stem the tide of depression during the 1920s had been ineffective. Cheaper credit for the farmers and higher tariffs were not the answer. However, the widely debated McNary-Haugen plan which sought to place a subsidy on wheat exports, and a similar export debenture plan, were unacceptable to Congress. Cooperative marketing that tried to give the farmers a larger share of the purchaser's dollar also was encouraged. It gained widespread approval with the enactment of the Agricultural Marketing Act of 1929 that provided for a Federal Farm Board which attempted to consolidate the grip of the farmers on the market and stabilize farm prices. The cooperatives deserved to be part of any long-range program to benefit the farmers, but they were not the immediate solution to huge surpluses, falling prices, heavy indebtedness, foreclosures, and widespread unrest. By 1932 these efforts had spent their force and another proposal, the domestic allotment plan of Milburn L. Wilson, calling for an adjustment of production to demand, began to attract attention.

Meanwhile, a relentless campaign was being waged in behalf of inflation. Henry A. Wallace advocated it before he became the new secretary of agriculture; so did the American Farm Bureau Federation and the National Farmers' Union. Even the Federal Farm Board, the Reconstruction Finance Corporation, and the Federal Reserve Board under Herbert Hoover had given it the green light; there also was clamor for it on Wall Street. By mid-April 1933, forty or more inflationary proposals were pending in Congress, the most popular being the old Populist formula for the free and unlimited coinage of silver. However, it soon became evident that the administration was going to give consideration to only two inflationary proposals: the devaluation of the dollar, and federal expenditures for a large public works program.

Simultaneously, farmers in Iowa who had been hard hit by the depression and had witnessed the banks declare "a holiday" by closing their doors, making it impossible for them to withdraw their money, began thinking about taking measures of their own. They began talking about "a farmers' buying, selling and taxpaying strike" unless effective measures were taken for their relief. In the earliest phases roads were blockaded, picket lines formed, and violence broke out; there were fights, gun-toting, the storming of jails and capital buildings, and the stopping of trains and automobiles. The grain and livestock farmers of the Middle West and the South, in particular, were urged to declare a holiday. If prices failed to reach a cost-of-production level within thirty days the farmers were to extend the strike to perishable products as well.

As 1932 turned into 1933 the strikers turned to the stoppage of farm evictions and the enactment of moratorium legislation that would prevent farm foreclosures. Meanwhile, the use of force continued. Forced farm sales were broken up in Wisconsin, Iowa, and Minnesota. The worst case of violence occurred when a mob of 600 broke into the court chambers of a presiding judge in Le Mars, Iowa, and demanded that he not execute any more foreclosures. When he refused, he was dragged from his courtroom, blindfolded, taken to a crossroads, and severely beaten and threatened with death.

UPI

Dispirited farmers listen as their land is sold at a public auction in Spotsylvania County, Virginia, in 1933. One-quarter of the county was sold at prices as low as 30 or 35 cents an acre.

Less than ten days after Roosevelt took office the Farm Holiday Association met in Des Moines under the motto that "The Farmer Feeds the World and Deserves His Pay." They passed resolutions demanding farm prices based on the cost of production; no foreclosures on rural or urban properties; and the reopening by the federal government of land held by insurance and mortgage companies for settlement by "actual homeowners." On May 12, 1933, the day the AAA became law, the farm holiday leaders postponed the strike called for May 13, but warned they would be watching the actions of the Roosevelt administration closely.

The AAA's Fair Prices Program

The Agricultural Adjustment Act (AAA) marked the beginning of a new era in agriculture. Its aim was to give fair or parity prices to farmers by granting benefit payments to the producers of basic commodities. These were limited at first to seven: cotton, wheat, corn, hogs, rice, tobacco, and milk and its products. They were later expanded to include the commodities of other producers if they agreed to adjust their production to demand and strive for parity

prices. To raise money and make benefit payments to the cooperating farmers, taxes were levied on those portions of the basic commodities selling below fair exchange values.

Henry A. Wallace, the new secretary of agriculture, was a controversial personality but well qualified for his new assignment, with an excellent reputation as a corn breeder, statistician, and mathematician. He knew the leading farm thinkers of the day and he expressed a willingness to try new methods and experiments. He also had a very good grasp of the relation of agriculture to the broader social and economic issues of the day.

Critics viewed Wallace as "a day-dreamer," an eccentric given to strange notions and ideas and prone to listen to impractical visionaries. Others who conceded his concern for the farmers asserted he cared more for the landlords than for tenants and sharecroppers, more for whites than for blacks. Still others who had been impressed with his reformist zeal during the initial stages of his administration were disappointed with his performance during

the second administration when he became involved with issues more far-reaching than those of the farmer. He was suspected of being more concerned with the availability of the Democratic nomination than he was with alleviating the plight of the farmers.

The situation of the cotton farmers and the hog producers was considered most urgent by the AAA. Contracts were drawn by the agency with cotton growers to withdraw about two-fifths of their land from production. By the late fall of 1933 the price of cotton was up three or four cents a pound over the previous year, despite the rise in costs.

Hog production was a more complicated problem. The market was glutted with the animals and an emergency program agreed upon the immediate removal of 2 billion pounds of pork from public consumption in 1933–34. The edible portion was sold or donated to relief agencies while the remainder was converted into lard and, if necessary, soap. Although many critics left the impression that food was being destroyed in complete disregard of human need, the emergency program was handled wisely. More than a million pounds of dry salt pork were distributed

The AAA, under Henry Wallace (pointing), purchased great quantities of hogs, usually reared on corn, to raise both corn and hog prices. Tobacco production (right) was also restricted to increase the farmers' return.

by early 1934 and some 22 million pounds of grease sold through the regular channels of trade by late 1933. A second program purchased 2 million hogs between November 1933 and September 1934 to be processed and distributed among families on relief rolls. It was likewise designed to remove surpluses from the market and support hog prices.

In the case of wheat, haste was unnecessary in 1933. The wheat crop that year was the smallest on record since 1894. Still, plans called for a reduction of the crops for 1934 and 1935 by 20 per cent. Conditions among the wheat growers, however, were still far from satisfactory. Prices of the goods and services they bought rose faster than the prices they received for their products. This was especially true in the spring wheat states of Minnesota, North and South Dakota, Montana, and Wisconsin. The winter wheat farmers of Kansas and other states in the southern tier of the wheat belt harvested their crop early and took advantage of the earlier, higher prices.

Dairy farmers faced a greater dilemma and were less prepared for the AAA than the other producers. There had been little support among the industry's rank and file for the new program. Inclusion of dairy products in the list of basic commodities had been largely a defensive measure taken by the organized dairy interests unsure of which direction to take.

Control of milk production, the phase of the AAA that attracted most attention, became a reality when a compromise was reached that both authorized an individual farm quota system and kept the market open for new producers to enter. The larger milk producers favored a marketing agreement to raise prices but the Consumer's Counsel and the legal division of the AAA viewed this with suspicion as a monopoly device. More than 200 marketing agreements had been received by the AAA at the end of 1933 but only 15 of them had been signed. Wallace responded to the milk producers' demands for the stabilization of dairy prices with government assistance. He advanced them $12 million to remove butter and cheese from the market but also warned that some plan for the control of production must be worked out.

The tobacco growers were more receptive to the AAA. The production of tobacco was controlled to a considerable degree throughout the world so the application of this principle did not appear as revolutionary to the tobacco growers as it did to the producers of other commodities. Still, the problems were complex. Twenty-five different types were grown in the United States, each with different characteristics and uses. The program finally decided upon proposals that the tobacco acreages for 1933, 1934, and 1935 be reduced to approximately one-half of the 1932 level. Grower participation for 1933–35 was impressive.

Farmers were divided into particular commodity groups and all treated the same by the administration. The blanket program for cotton, hogs, wheat, dairy products, and other commodities contained no special provision to meet the needs of the small submarginal farmer. The tenants and sharecroppers fared badly under the AAA largely because there was no precedent in the colleges of agriculture, the Extension Service, or the Department of Agriculture for assisting such marginal producers. Further, the AAA programs were built around commodities rather than people, and advances in technology made it still easier and cheaper to disregard the human element and force the unfortunates off the land.

There was, finally, the widespread belief that there were too many people on the land and that many would be better served if they migrated to the cities.

The failure to come sufficiently to the assistance of the tenants and sharecroppers was largely responsible for the battle between the "agrarians" and "urban-liberals" within the AAA. The general counsel to the AAA, Jerome Frank, was the articulate urban-liberal spokesman. He maintained that under the terms of the 1934–35 contract the landlords had to retain the same number of tenants and sharecroppers on their farms as in the previous year. The landlord, according to Frank, entered into a contract with the government in which he agreed to reduce his crop, receive payment for it, retain the same number of tenants and sharecroppers on the farm, and share some of the benefits he received from the government with them. The agrarians, who reflected the views of the landlords, saw the contract in narrower legalistic terms. They argued that it was strictly an agreement between the landlord and the government. The landlord was to operate as he thought best and, if necessary, he could lay off sharecroppers or reduce them to hired laborers.

There was sharp reaction to this unfortunate state of affairs. The Southern Tenant Farmers' Union was organized in July 1934, amid growing criticism of the AAA cotton program and its administration, to help give the tenants and sharecroppers some bargaining power with the planters and to stop evictions and guarantee them their rights under the cotton contract. This controversy came to a head early in February 1935 when Chester C. Davis, the head of the AAA, with the approval of Wallace, asked for the resignation of Jerome Frank and some of his collaborators as a result of their liberal policies in 1934–35.

Help for the Small Farmer

The formation of the Resettlement Administration (RA), the predecessor of the Farm Security Administration (FSA), was in part a response to the need to do more for the sharecroppers and tenants, and also an answer to those who charged that the Federal Emergency Relief Administration (FERA) administered by Harry Hopkins was more urban-oriented than rural. Critics felt that the farm population was not faring as well as it should.

The RA took the position that big farmers were not the only people deserving federal help. Aid was to be given directly to the poorest elements of the farming community. Opposition was immediate and strong: Rex Tugwell, the new administrator, was disliked and distrusted by farm spokesmen when he proclaimed the principles of the RA which appeared to be contrary to those of the AAA. And the new agency was further handicapped

by the fact that the rural elements it sought to aid were the least influential in the country.

It took a tragedy of immense proportions to offer a glimmer of hope to the cause of the disinherited. Farm mismanagement and drought brought disaster to the Great Plains and neighboring areas in the middle of the decade. Bankrupt small farmers, shareholders, and tenants—the Oakies and the Arkies—packed up for California and other Pacific Coast states. Presidential recognition of the situation was made official when the Special Committee on Farm Tenancy was appointed by Roosevelt. And when Congress passed the Bankhead-Jones Act in 1937 and the Farm Security Administration was established it seemed to suggest that better days were ahead for the poorer farmer and his family.

Unfortunately passage of this Bankhead-Jones Act served only to demonstrate that Congress and the administration had little sympathy with the communal farm idea

The Resettlement Administration served the poorest elements of rural America. Ben Shahn's poster graphically illustrates the agony of cropless years in the Dust Bowl.

Although the New Deal failed to please all farming interests, it did attempt to tackle the rural predicament of overproduction and falling incomes. Left: A South Dakota man pauses outside Missoula, Montana, on his journey west. Below: Ohio farmers debate the government's agricultural policies in 1938.

121

The Dust Bowl

The wind blows up out of the Gulf through the natural bowl formed by the panhandles of Texas and Oklahoma and continues around the adjoining parts of Kansas, Colorado, and New Mexico. It blows almost without pause, yet brings only fifteen inches of rain to the treeless plains every year. Only the short and tightly woven prairie grass holds the earth close and conserves the moisture.

When the delicate balance of wind and rain and grass was upset in the nineteenth century by overgrazing, the plains responded dramatically. The huge herds of beef cattle and sheep were culled by drought and blizzard. Then men stripped the sod away to establish great wheat "factories," but the wind only blew harder and drier until, in the 1930s, the fertility was blown out of the desiccated land and the area became known as the Dust Bowl.

When the price of wheat fell from a dollar to seventy cents a bushel in 1930, the plains farmers tried to maintain their income by simply growing more wheat. More land was plowed up even though the number of wheat acres harvested had already trebled in the 1920s. If prices were to be low then it had to be quantity. The next spring saw the greatest yield ever. Fields that commonly produced twelve bushels now produced fifty—with devastating effect. Prices plummeted to twenty cents a bushel. About 40 per cent of the crop was never even sent to market. The *New York Times* noted in August, "It is difficult to describe what has been done to the farmer economically, and in hope, spirit, and morale." It seemed the land was reaping its own harvest of neglect, but the men of the plains were oblivious. The price, they thought, had to rise—more land was planted in the fall of 1932.

Cold, disease, and finally drought ruined that crop and brought farmers to their knees. Mortgages were called. Wheat "kings" collapsed. The rest began a wild orgy of reckless plowing in an effort to pay the creditors. Cattle died, cows went dry, and hogs were too thin for any buyer: the golden era of the plains was over.

In the fall of 1933 farmers planted in soil that was little more than powder. There had never been so little rain on so much bare land. And the land was exhausted. Years of one-crop farming had used up the organic matter which once bound the soil. The constant, ever-

present wind began to turn the soil to sand and then to dust. On April 14, 1934, the first great storm came—and whole fields moved. The sand penetrated everywhere and into everything. Rabbits and other small animals suffocated in the swirling dust. Darkness reigned for forty minutes under a great, swirling black cloud.

On May 10, a different kind of storm swept the topsoil into the air to a height of 15,000 feet. The sun was obscured from the Dakotas to Texas. The very land was being carried away—enough of it to darken the sky on the East Coast for five hours. Twelve million tons of the plains fell on Chicago alone. Two days later, a ship 300 miles off New York radioed for an explanation of the falling dust.

The rains came later that month and there was a brief collective sigh of relief, but within days the situation was as bad as ever. The sand drifted into dunes as high as thirty feet. Houses were buried, fields were choked or had craters whipped out of them by the wind. "Despite all the wind and the dust," remembered one Oklahoma farmer, "we were putting in crops but making no crops. . . . We made five crop failures in five years." And it worsened. The soil simply disappeared in the face of gusts up to sixty miles an hour in February of 1935. Boulders were uncovered in fields and stood as monuments to the fury of the abused land. Pipelines once two feet underground reappeared. The Rock Island Railroad had to bring in crews to shovel out a path to California.

Tens of thousands of farmers headed west. Some counties in the Dust Bowl lost 60 per cent of their population during these years. Families packed up their belongings on whatever transport was available and headed away from the "black blizzards."

The drought ended in 1937 and the last years of the decade saw the rehabilitation of the plains by massive federal aid programs. Soil conservation was demonstrated, millions of acres were replanted with grass, and innumerable rows of trees planted to block the wind. But it was too late for the thousands living a nomadic existence in the orchards and fields of faraway states. As one "Okie" said, "This is a hard life to swallow but I just couldn't sit there and look to someone to feed us."

Fierce winds wreaked havoc in the great plains during the 1930s. Neglect and drought loosened the soil and the winds carried it away. Arthur Rothstein photographed an Oklahoma farmer and his two boys fleeing such a storm in Cimarron County in 1936.

of the Southern Tenant Farmers' Union. The act also made clear that progress toward farm ownership by tenants through the FSA was going to be slow, "a sop" at best. Between 2,500 and 3,000 tenants could be financed for ownership with FSA appropriations during the first year —about one farm for each county in the United States. At the rate the FSA was progressing, according to one estimate, it was going to take 400 years to make farm owners of the tenants of the country. On the other hand, the failure of the FSA to make the kind of speedy progress that many hoped it would make should not obscure the fact that it did help many small, destitute farmers whom the AAA did not assist with credit, advice on better farming methods, medical care, and other needs.

The New Deal, through the Rural Electrification Administration, made remarkable strides in furnishing electricity to even the most inaccessible areas. Livestock and crop production were improved. Indoor plumbing and wider use of machinery became possible. Electricity also brought cheaper labor costs, an extension of the working day, and daily contact with the outside world through the use of the radio.

Soil conservation became a key objective after the first AAA had been declared unconstitutional, although it had been encouraged from the beginning in a secondary sort of way. The Soil Conservation and Domestic Allotment Act of 1936 placed emphasis on increasing the

The FSA enabled nearly 40,000 families to buy their own farms. Above: FSA clients listen to a farm lecture near Marshall, Texas, in 1937. Right: A tenant farmer helped by the administration poses for a photograph with his three sons in Caruthersville, Missouri, in 1938.

The Ever-Normal Granary scheme constructed storage facilities and purchased crops in years of abundance to help stabilize farm prices. Right Iowa bins for shelled corn, photographed in 1939.

income of the farmers through the adoption of land uses and farm practices that conserved and built up the fertility of the soil. However, the favorable conditions of 1937 and the prospects of excellent crops in 1938 stressed the need for a broader program based on the control of large reserves and their storage. The AAA of 1938 sought to meet this need with the establishment of the Ever-Normal Granary to provide for these reserves and bring protection from drought.

A big issue facing the AAA during the late 1930s concerned who should be in charge of the programs. While local leaders preferred practical men—those who knew how to speak the language of the farmers—the land grant colleges spoke for the more professional men of the Extension Service or farm management groups. The successor of Chester Davis as administrator of the AAA, Howard Ross Tolley, was representative of the latter group. He was a somber, apolitical man, academic in his approach and insensitive to the clamor of politicians. Greater farmer participation was viewed as an answer to the charge of bureaucracy and as part of the broader effort to strengthen democracy at a time when other nations were abandoning it. This argument had great appeal in an age terrorized by dictators. But the more suspicious viewed this as part of the grand design to help Henry A. Wallace win the Democratic nomination in 1940 if Roosevelt decided not to run for a third term.

Wallace's program was thrown into confusion by the heavy loss of supporting congressmen in the hog and wheat states in the election of 1938, which reflected farmer dissatisfaction with low prices and AAA controls. AAA officials wanted to retain the control features of the AAA of 1938, but make them more effective. Meanwhile many bills had been introduced embracing further monetary changes, export subsidies, rigid government price-fixing, unlimited protection, tariff revision, and other proposals.

Criticisms of the New Deal's handling of the farmers and their problems abounded. But the truth is that some of these problems were beyond the powers of any one nation and her leaders to resolve. Some transcended national boundary lines, and even those that were within the power of the nation and her leaders to repair could not be undone within a short time. They had been years in the making and would be years in the unmaking. The Farm Security Administration, the Bankhead-Jones Act, crop insurance, the Ever-Normal Granary were just beginning to gather pace when the New Deal ended.

Farmers with capital and resources probably had more to gain from the New Deal than those without them. The New Deal helped revive and maintain the morale of the farmers after one of the greatest falls in history. Even though most farm prices had not risen to parity levels when the New Deal came to an end, they were higher than they had been in 1932–33; and the New Deal as well as inclement weather deserve credit for their rise. Both farmers and the general public became more sensitive to the need for conservation as a result of New Deal programs. A laudable beginning was made in furnishing electricity to rural areas. Finally, statesmanlike measures, such as the reciprocal trade treaties, were bravely but futilely adopted in an attempt to unclog the channels of international trade. The New Deal, with all its limitations in attempting to lighten the burdens of the farmers during the Great Depression, constituted one of the most constructive periods in the history of American agriculture.

Chapter 6

PRESERVING THE AMERICAN SYSTEM

Despite the clear endorsement he had received at the polls in 1936, Roosevelt seemed to have lost the overwhelming support of earlier years. The long honeymoon had ended. Dissension appeared in the ranks of the Democratic party over New Deal policies, and the recurrence of recession in 1937 caused widespread unease. Seven million people remained jobless, and the 1938 midterm election results delivered a stinging rebuff to the president. In 1939, concerned at ominous developments abroad, Roosevelt called a halt to domestic reform. After six years of feverish activity, what had the New Deal achieved? And what principles had guided Roosevelt in his actions on behalf of the nation?

The Second New Deal

The Democratic platform of 1936 had been outspoken and eloquent: "We hold this truth to be self-evident; that government in a modern civilization has certain inescapable obligations to its citizens, among which are: 1. Protection of the family and the home; 2. The establishment of a democracy of opportunity for all people; 3. Aid to those overtaken by disaster." To this now conventional New Dealism, Roosevelt had added the famous remark expressing the new militancy of 1936—the promise to "rid our land of kidnappers, bandits and malefactors of great wealth." In his second inaugural, delivered in January 1937, he called attention to "One-third of a nation ill-housed, ill-clad, ill-nourished," and made clear that the New Deal would continue. Indeed it was a statement of a broad and coordinated plan of social and economic reform.

The high hopes of 1936, however, were to be disappointed. Very little legislation was passed in 1937 and the legislative achievements for that year were only partial and meager. The attack on the malefactors of great wealth led to the establishment of a joint congressional-executive committee to gather evidence on monopolistic trends. It was rich in documentation but feeble in achievement. The extension of social security was postponed, and was indeed not enacted fully until the advent of President Truman's Fair Deal. And, not least, the attack on the Supreme Court brought a split between those who trusted and those who distrusted the president. It did great harm to the Democratic party and to relations between the president and Congress.

Nevertheless, some important economic reform measures were enacted in these years. In 1936 the Securities Exchange Commission was given new responsibilities under the Public Utility Holding Act, by which all utility companies were compelled to register with the SEC and to give it full information on all their operations. The commission was now to see that each company limited its activities to a single well-integrated system. But this "death sentence law" against holding companies did of course add to the bitter antagonism toward the president and many utility corporations fought it with tooth and claw. Nevertheless, it was upheld by the Supreme Court in 1938 and was genuinely effective.

In 1937 the Rural Electrification Administration was given extended powers. It was not authorized to build its own power generating plants but to encourage the formation of cooperative groups of farmers who would buy electricity from existing sources. By 1944 nearly 1,000 farmers' cooperatives for this purpose had been set up and electricity lines were winding into remote communities from Vermont to Oregon. In 1925 only 4 per cent of the country's farms had electricity. By 1940 the figure had risen to 25 per cent.

In 1937 the United States Housing Administration was established. Federal aid was provided to local and state governments by long term and low interest loans, for the purpose of slum clearance and the building of low cost housing. Again, if the program was not as successful as ardent New Dealers had hoped, there were still 300 housing projects begun by 1939.

The Farm Security Administration was also set up in 1937. But as with the USHA, this program fell short of the expectations in Roosevelt's original program for enhancing the economic position of tenant farmers. The second AAA was enacted in 1938 and replaced the act of 1933 which had been declared unconstitutional. The measures it introduced failed to reduce the 1939 crop surplus, while in subsequent years demands from war-torn Europe outbalanced supply.

The Fair Labor Standards Act, Congress's answer to the recommended program for the regulation of hours and wages, was passed in 1938. (A similar bill had been defeated in June 1937, being the first major New Deal bill to be rejected by Congress.) National standards of a 44-hour maximum week and a 25-cent hourly minimum wage were established for industries engaged in interstate commerce. These standards were gradually raised until they became, in 1940, a 40-hour week and a 40-cent hourly wage. Over 300,000 workers received increased wages and/or shorter hours under this measure. This was a major reform, but even so, it had been watered down from the original bill presented to Congress, and had only barely been passed.

It was an impressive legislative record. The labor force was making use of the Wagner Act, the farmers were reassured by the Conservation and Domestic Allotment Act. An act was passed in 1936 to give the country a maritime fleet worthy of its strength, and even the bitter campaign of Republicans and Democrats alike against the president's "Court-packing bill," and the great debate on it which raged through the spring and summer of 1937, were by no means ineffective in persuading the Court in the end to reverse itself and to hand down favorable decisions upon a number of New Deal measures. As the cynics of the day put it: "A switch in time saves nine."

Yet the grim fact remained that the president who had won so great a personal triumph in 1936 was fifteen months later having to fight for all the measures he valued, and not always successfully. The days of his open and happy dictatorship were now over. The evidence of this was not only in the campaign to reform the Supreme Court but in the storm raised by his proposals for authority to reorganize the civil service. There was little in them that was especially novel, yet little here was enacted and most of the major reforms that the president asked for had to wait for the Hoover Commission of 1946–47 before they could be implemented. He now met

The photographs on this and the following two pages
are taken from some of the 270,000 negatives filed
by a group of about twelve distinguished photographers working for the FSA in the 1930s. Above:
A dejected, jobless man slouches against a vacant
shop (by Dorothea Lange). Top: Missouri families
roam through California in search of work, 1936
(Lange). Top left: Two farmers chat in the shade
during the 1936 drought (Lange). Left: Cheerful
survivors of the drought of 1930–31 (uncredited).

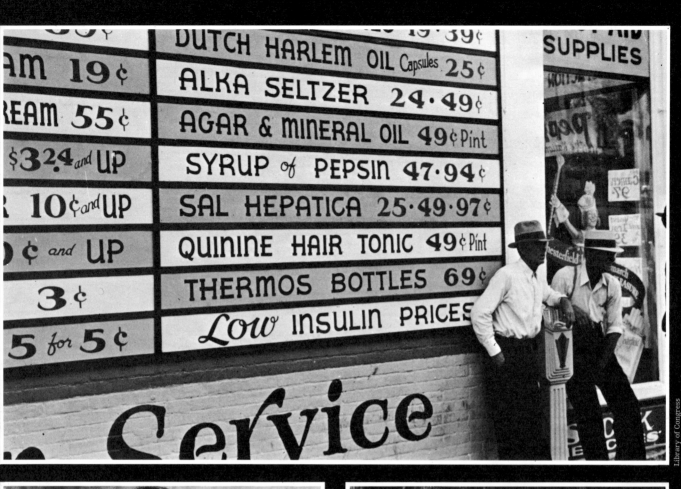

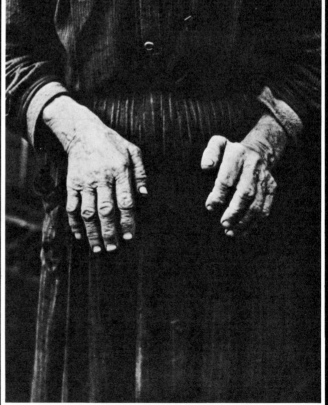

Top left: A drugstore sign in Newark, Ohio, 1938 (by Ben Shahn). Above: Laborers children who had never attended school, Oklahoma, 1939 (Russell Lee). Far left: Migrant mother, 1936 (Dorothea Lange). Center: The gnarled hands of a homesteader (Lee). Left: On US 40 in central Ohio, 1938 (Shahn).

The Wagner-Steagall Act of 1937 established the USHA to improve housing conditions of low-income groups. Above: A WPA poster praises a new housing project in Ohio.

opposition on many fronts. Catholics were aroused, especially by Father Coughlin, to the alleged danger of federal control of parochial schools. Financial purists were worried by the apparent threat to the independence of the comptroller general, and horsemen in appropriate costume rode from Boston dressed as minutemen and modern Paul Reveres to arouse the country to the charge that that man in the White House was now clearly a tyrant in disguise. By 1938, in the face of this mounting wave of discontent, the president began to talk to his closest friends of his intention to retire at the end of his second term. He intimated to Louis Howe and to Harry Hopkins that the democratic nomination in 1940 was open. What were the roots of this malaise? Why was the New Deal apparently running out of steam?

The man now clearly had enemies. At a Jackson Day Dinner in 1936 he dwelt on the comparison with Jackson, and used the phrase that the people loved him "for the

enemies he had made." He was ready now to identify his own enemies, and some had been his friends and allies. "The old Roosevelt magic has lost its kick," former NRA administrator Hugh Johnson said, with malice, in the spring of 1938. "The diverse elements of his Falstaffian army can no longer be kept together and led by a melodious whinny and a winning smile." There was nothing new in the hatred the rich felt for him. And there was little new in the publicity that his family received: the attacks on his children; the charge in the *Saturday Evening Post* that his son James had exploited his family connections to obtain insurance business; all the spite, gossip, and amusement occasioned by Eleanor Roosevelt's daily columns in the press. Opinion polls in the spring of 1938, however, still showed that eight out of ten Americans liked FDR as a personality. They showed also that the blacks, the poor in general, the ranks of labor and the unemployed were for him enthusiastically. The Southwest as a section was 98 per cent for him personally, but fewer than half of those polled expressed support for his economic goals, and more than half were either opposed to them or uninformed about them. Of five major economic groups—the blacks, the poor, the lower middle-class, the upper middle-class and the prosperous—all but the first two showed majorities against his methods. Running through this opposition there was now a genuine streak of fear at his apparent bid for political power. Half of those polled thought that he had too much power, and as a consequence of dictatorship in Europe there was a great deal of talk of the danger of dictatorship at home. On Capitol Hill, this sentiment took the form of distaste for his controversial legislation, distaste for government by crises and talk of crises, and in particular distaste for the nonelected zealots who surrounded him; the do-gooders, academics, and economic pundits who were running a "Phi Beta Kappa Tammany Hall."

Divisions among the Democrats

This mood affected his own party. There was clearly now an anti-New Deal group, including Vice President Garner, and senators like Josiah Bailey of North Carolina, Harry Byrd of Virginia, Millard Tydings of Maryland, and Royal Copeland of New York. The violent battle over the Supreme Court had helped to split the party for the first time since the beginning of the New Deal. Senators Burton Wheeler and Carter Glass, formerly leaders of the New Deal program, went over to the opposition on this issue, and subsequently felt free to vote against other legislative proposals made by or for Roosevelt. They were followed in this action by other New Deal supporters. The Supreme Court battle also lost Roosevelt the influential backing of several progressive Republicans, including

Senators George Norris, Hiram Johnson, and William Borah, who had previously supported the domestic policies of the New Deal.

To all this difficulty there has to be added the impact of the recession of 1937. There had been a slow, steady upswing of the business cycle from 1933 to 1937, but suddenly, in the late summer of 1937, a reversal set in which has been termed the Roosevelt Recession. In part it was due to federal cutbacks in the spending program, especially in WPA budgets, in part to the government's apparent distrust of business. During this business decline, which lasted for twelve months, stocks dropped, the national income dwindled, unemployment rose, and industrial production fell off. The New Deal was caught unawares, and its leaders did not understand what the trouble could be, for there had been none of the stock-market speculation, overproduction, or overexpansion of credit which had preceded the crash of 1929.

The recession was a challenge to Roosevelt for a number of reasons. It seemed clear that the New Deal had not gone far enough. Despite the alphabet of agencies, the mass spending, and the mass liberal and radical waves of protest, there were still over 7 million unemployed. The National Resources Committee, an executive fact-finding agency, revealed that 59 per cent of all American families had annual cash incomes of less than $1,250, and 81 per cent of less than $2,000. If the goals of the New Deal were not only prosperity but some measure of distributive justice—and many of its advocates made this claim—it had failed to reach these families. Progressivism was not enough, said Rex Tugwell: "It was in economics that our troubles lay." There was an obvious need, once again, for the president to spend his way out of adversity. But by 1938 not all his advisers were agreed on this. There were those, like Henry Morgenthau, Jr who wanted to balance the budget and made plain their demands for government economy. There were those, like Thurman Arnold, campaigning for an attack on the economic royalists and the busting of the trusts. And there was the central and dominant Keynesian group led by Secretary of the Interior Harold Ickes, Henry Wallace, Frances Perkins and, now most influential of all, Harry Hopkins. There were rising stars, too, products of Harvard Law School and protégés of Supreme Court Justice Felix Frankfurter, in the eyes of Hearst's newspapers "The Iago of the Administration": shy Ben Cohen from Muncie, Indiana; the bubbling Tommy Corcoran (Tommy the Cork), adept at Irish jokes and good with his accordion; William O. Douglas, the sandy-haired ex-professor, now chairman of the SEC who was later to become a Supreme Court judge and live a long and much-married life; and Robert Jackson. To Hugh Johnson, they were "White House Janizaries"—a palace guard of acolytes.

Among them all the president dickered. His friends pleaded for a reassertion of his moral leadership. "Mr

President", wrote Wallace, "you must furnish that firm and confident leadership which made you such a joy to the nation in March 1933." What finally moved the president was the steady drop in the stock market, especially in the spring of 1938—a drop from the previous September that was the sharpest the country had ever known. In mid-April he moved, and put forward to Congress a $3 million public works spending program; he carried the same message to the nation in a long fireside chat. Two weeks later he launched a thorough study of the concentration of economic power in American industry, and the effect of that concentration on the decline of competition. Washington recognized the signs. By 1938 the phrase was, "Moley is in opposition; Tugwell is in the city planning business; Hugh Johnson is in a rage."

Paradoxically, the "New New Deal" suffered from the fact that the Democrats enjoyed an excessive majority in Congress. It is an axiom of American, or of any democratic, politics that when no substantial organized political opposition is ready to step in and take over from the party in power, the incentive for party unity in the latter is lacking. In 1937 the Republican party had almost collapsed. The Republicans who had survived the New Deal landslide were, with some exceptions, undistinguished figures incapable of directing an effective political opposition. There was no obvious need for unity in the diverse Democratic coalition and many dissident Democrats, especially from the South, hated Roosevelt more than they hated their Republican opponents. These men began to form a working coalition with northern Republicans against the Roosevelt bloc. The group was often joined by some middle-class liberals, who were tired of reform and even fearful of the consequences of what they had already done to further the New Deal program.

A Decline in Roosevelt's Influence

As the congressional elections of 1938 drew near, it was clear that the president intended to seek to discipline his large but divided party. James Farley, "the man with the beckoning finger," advised him that the wisest course of discipline would be closer consultation between the White House and Capitol Hill, and a more skillful use of patronage. It was clear indeed that there was a wide gap between the White House and the Hill, and increasingly less consultation between the two branches of the federal government. But Farley's advice was ignored. In Georgia, Maryland, and New York the president openly supported candidates who were trying to unseat the sitting members. He wanted, he said, to get rid of those who deep in their hearts did not believe in New Deal "principles." In Kentucky he threw

FDR's brisk and colorful ways gave cartoonists great scope in the 1930s and, ultimately, made it easy to encapsulate his early career in their work. In the inauguration parade of 1933. Herbert Hoover looks doubtful about FDR's public assurance in Peter Arno's illustration (above left). Clifford Berryman sketched the president a year later as a doctor dispensing the alphabet agencies cure (left). The president's grandchildren protested his fireside verbosity in Rodney Sarro's cartoon of 1935 (above). And Nat Collier's anti-New Deal illustration (right) during the campaign of 1936 suggested that Roosevelt had been telling unlikely tales.

his influence on the side of Senator Barkley (later President Truman's vice president) who was fighting desperately against the energetic Governor "Happy" Chandler. In state after state he sought to purge anti-New Deal Democrats from Congress by appealing directly to the people for their defeat. In this he was imitating his one-time hero Woodrow Wilson, who had similarly intervened in the congressional elections of 1918. He met the same result. In the South, where the need for it was greatest, the purge suffered a sorry defeat. Senators Walter George of Georgia, Millard Tydings of Maryland, "Cotton Ed" Smith of South Carolina, and others easily won reelection. Even before the Republican victory in the congressional elections, it was clear that the New Deal was in deep trouble.

It is true there were still overwhelming Democratic majorities in both Houses. The Republicans lost twenty-four of the thirty-two Senate contests. Blacks, Poles, Italians, and the unions were now solidly Democratic. But there were striking Republican gains, eight in the Senate, eighty-one in the House, and thirteen new governorships. In New York, Governor Herbert Lehman, the brilliant vote-getter, only just managed to defeat the youthful Republican candidate Thomas E. Dewey. In Ohio, the Republican John W. Bricker defeated the Democratic governor, and Robert Taft defeated a capable New Deal senator, Ian Black. Democrats lost control of the state government of Pennsylvania. In Michigan Governor Murphy was punished for his alleged tolerance of sit-down strikes, and in Connecticut Governor Cross was punished for his intolerance toward them. It was not only the Democratic party that was suffering; the candidates the president supported were defeated, and the candidates he denounced as "Copperheads" were triumphantly elected. There were only two exceptions, in Kentucky where Senator Alban Barkley was re-elected, and in New York City where Representative John O'Connor was narrowly defeated. Although Democrats retained control of both Houses, their majorities in 1938 were so reduced that for the first time in five years the Republican party could operate as an effective minority.

There was a further reason for the decline in the president's reputation. It is true that the New Deal had conspicuously given some measure of recognition to the unions. But economic recovery and the growing union strength encouraged a division in the ranks of labor and produced a wave of public alarm at union strength. In November 1938, when the AFL and CIO split, the president sought successfully to arbitrate between them. John L. Lewis for his part was highly critical of what he called the excessive loyalty of most union leaders to the president. The few remaining Republican leaders, like William Hutcheson of the carpenters, shared his views, and in the CIO Communist infiltration won some influence for members or for friends of the Communist party, like

A California worker proudly holds his union book in 1938. John L. Lewis led the CIO in drives to unionize workers by industry rather than by craft, as the AFL continued to do.

Harry Bridges of the longshoremen of the West Coast. The strength of the labor movement and the character of the contentious John L. Lewis as its leader, were proving to be a source not of strength but of weakness in the uneasy Democratic coalition.

In January 1939, Roosevelt, concerned about the threat of world war, called a halt to his domestic reform program:

We have now passed the period of internal conflict in the launching of our program of social reform. Our full energies may now be released to invigorate the processes of recovery in order to preserve our reforms, and to give every man and woman who wants to work a real job at a living wage. . . . But this is of paramount importance. The deadline of danger from within and from without is not within our control. The hour-glass may be in the hands of other nations. Our own hour-glass tells us that we are off on a race to make democracy work, so that we may be efficient in peace and therefore secure in national defense.

In seeming tip-top spirits, FDR parries questions from behind the steering wheel in Warm Springs, Georgia, in April 1939. But the jaunty pose and broad smile belied a deep concern for the growing world crisis.

AP

A Balanced Political Program

How then does one assess the New Deal as a whole? It is of course clear that Roosevelt was first and last a supreme politician, and that his various experiments were based primarily on considerations of political opportunism. It can certainly be argued that the New Deal had no consistent policy or far-seeing plans and that the president's major desire was to win the support of the majority by giving to each group in the country enough of what it wanted. He had no coherent plan to replace the capitalist system: his role was that of the genial arbiter, the deft conciliator, the arch political manipulator. If he had an objective it was a return to the lost world of the 1920s, before booms and slumps destroyed the prosperity that capitalism brought. For this purpose Roosevelt, the Brain Trusters, and the Democratic politicians in general wished to win and hold the support of a diverse coalition: of conservative southern Democrats, of the labor groups on the Left, of the big-city machine politicians, of the anti-monopoly western wing with its folk memories of Bryan and Populism. All deserved something from the New Deal, and no single one could get everything it wished. The president had to walk a tightrope among them all, and

use it also to bind them all to him and to his cause. Or, to use another analogy, he had to keep his ear close to the ground—even if grasshoppers sometimes jumped in.

In general, the New Deal followed the political philosophy, expressed by Vice President Garner in 1938, that it was foolish to talk of dividing the nation into two opposing political camps, progressive and conservative, or to crusade for "causes," because any party in the United States which serves the nation must necessarily be a coalition of diverse interests. It was in large part the failure of the Republicans to take more diverse and progressive elements into their party during this period that caused them to lose elections. Given this assumption, based largely upon the nature of the American party system, the strategy, if not the philosophy, was clear. The New Deal was neither Left nor Right, and Roosevelt skillfully sailed a zig-zag course in accordance with the conditions of political wind and weather. In the 1932 campaign he criticized Hoover for extravagance. In 1938 he charged that Hoover had failed to spend enough to fight the depression. Consistency is a rare, and perhaps even a "non-political," gift.

But if for FDR the theory of political opportunism is valid, this theory fails to recognize that there were consistent themes underlying the New Deal. One important aspect was its essential humanitarianism; Roosevelt

OURS...to fight for

Freedom of Speech

EACH ACCORDING TO THE DICTATES OF HIS OWN CONSCIENCE

NORMAN ROCKWELL

Freedom of Worship

Freedom from Want

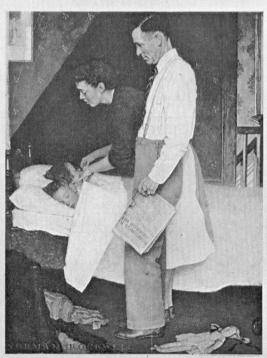

Freedom from Fear

loved people in the concrete sense and not in the abstract, and was deeply interested in their problems and needs, their psychological quirks, their liabilities and potential. No person, great or modest, escaped his interest and concern; like President Jackson, FDR considered himself a tribune of the people. He felt a responsibility to all the groups in the community. His interest in "the forgotten man" was clear. Provisions in the WPA program provided for occupational groups, like artists and writers, who were not usually considered in such government programs. Other legislation benefited minority groups, who exerted no direct political power, like the tenant farmers, the 12 million negroes in the US, and not least, the youth of the nation. As Frances Perkins, Roosevelt's secretary of labor, put it, his central belief was that people mattered.

Roosevelt was a political realist who had come to see, as had many others in this period, that in the twentieth century, political stability rested upon economic security. Political and social democracy were impossible as long as there were conditions of mass unemployment and widespread want in the midst of potential plenty. It is significant that in his famous Four Freedoms speech (January 1941) FDR added to the two negative freedoms of worship and the press, which are rights against interference from the government, two new and positive freedoms—from want and fear—which concern the right of protection against economic insecurity and military aggression. He accepted that the government had an obligation to secure both these positive freedoms. There was more to it than James Madison or Thomas Jefferson had foreseen: that government was no longer necessarily best that governs least. In a fireside chat of 1938, he stated that democracy had disappeared in many other nations of the world, because the people had grown tired of hunger and insecurity while their governments did nothing, and that they had chosen to sacrifice liberty in return for something to eat. He believed that a government must accept the responsibility of providing economic security for its people, if social and economic democracy are to be preserved. On a smaller scale, the Hoover administration had begun gradually and reluctantly to move in this same direction, but the New Deal accepted this new theory of government responsibility for general welfare cheerfully and vigorously, and executed it in full measure. By 1938 Roosevelt's thinking had taken a new direction. He was seeing his enemy clearly now, and was sometimes being called a traitor to his class for doing so. Private power, he said, was "stronger than the democratic state itself." In the United States "a concentration of private power without equal in history is growing,"

Norman Rockwell's poster illustrates Roosevelt's "Four Freedoms" speech. FDR had added freedom from want and fear to the freedom of speech and worship proclaimed in the Constitution.

which was "seriously impairing the effectiveness of private enterprise." Indeed, that private enterprise "is ceasing to be free enterprise and is becoming a cluster of private collectivisms." And "Big business collectivism in industry compels an ultimate collectivism in government."

Given this recognition of government responsibilities and of its range, the New Deal sought to create an economic balance between the different major economic groups of the nation, so that by protecting and aiding them in a significant way, the natural operation of the economy would be restored. Business was aided by the NRA, and by the reciprocal-trade program, which stimulated world trade and increased America's share of the world market. The farmers got the AAA and FSA. Labor was given the NLRA and the Fair Labor Standards Act. The unemployed were given the work and relief projects, and with others, they shared in the benefits of the social security program. These programs of support were based not on political opportunism alone, but on the basic theory that by the subsidizing of each group, the whole economy would operate more efficiently.

A Triumph for Big Government

Reacting in part to the rise in the twentieth century of big business and big labor, the US under the New Deal turned to big government, paralleling a similar development in other nations of the Western world. With this, the economic center of the US shifted from New York to Washington, DC as the federal government increasingly took over a major, perhaps the primary, role in directing American economic life. After a tour of the US in 1935, Sir Josiah Stamp the British economist wrote, "Just as in 1929 the whole country was Wall-Street-conscious, now it is Washington-conscious." The government became at once the partner of business, making loans through the RFC, and also the competitor of business, through the TVA. Myriad new powers were taken on by government. It began to manage the currency and it became the nation's largest banker, not only making business loans through the RFC but also making loans for housing and slum-clearance projects through the HOLC and to farmers through the FSA. The social security and the serviceman's insurance scheme made the federal government the nation's largest insurance salesman. Electric power was produced and sold, as well as fertilizers and other products, under the TVA. The government stored agricultural surpluses and subsidized American drama, fine arts, and motion pictures under the WPA. The program for the conservation of natural resources begun by Theodore Roosevelt was enlarged. Taxing, spending, lending, building, regulating —all became the functions of big government.

The consequence was a dramatic personalization of

federal government. Under Hoover, one man in the White House handled the mail; under FDR it took fifty. It meant more than the government interfering in and directing the economy. Twice-weekly press conferences with up to 200 reporters, ranging wide in their unscripted and unrehearsed questions, helped bring the president into the home. The persistent feeding of news items, and fireside chats over the radio, ensured that it was, despite its scale, government with a human face. As he spoke on the radio, "his head would nod and his hands would move in simple, natural, comfortable gestures," Frances Perkins recalled. "His face would smile and light up as though he were actually sitting on the front porch or in the parlor with them." Eleanor Roosevelt later observed that after the president's death people would stop her on the street to say "they missed the way the president used to talk to them. They'd say 'He used to talk to me about my government.' There was a real dialogue between Franklin and the people," she reflected. "That dialogue seems to have disappeared from the government since he died." The man was loved—and hated—throughout the US.

The practice of deficit financing, by which the government spent more than it took in taxes, was a major feature of the New Deal. In this, New Dealers operated on the Keynesian theory that, during a depression, the economy should be stimulated by the injection of mass purchasing power at the lowest level. The consequence was an enormous increase in the public debt. The First World War had caused a jump from slightly over $1 billion to more than $23 billion. The latter figure was reduced by over $6 billion through the economy measures of the 1920s, but in the depression years of Hoover's administration the debt again increased to $22.5 billion. The eight years of the New Deal saw an increase of some $25 billion, although this increase resulted in large part from the expenses of the rearmament and defense program of 1939–41. The years of the Second World War caused the astonishing increase of over $210 billion, to $260 billion. Thus, however costly the New Deal might have seemed to contemporaries, the cost of the Second World War caused an increase in the public debt which was more than eight times that of the cost of the New Deal.

The pronouncements of certain New Dealers, the relative speed with which the program was executed, and the scale of public spending gave the appearance of a revolution. In fact it was essentially conservative. Most New Deal acts had deep roots in American history—in the reform movements of the nineteenth century, in the Populist movement, and in the Progressive Era of Theodore Roosevelt and Woodrow Wilson. The administrations of Harding, Coolidge, and Hoover—not the New Deal—now appear as aberrations from the American economic stream: The New Deal did not attack capitalism, but saved it; by reforming capitalism it warded off social-

ism. From one point of view it can be seen as a failure. It was unable to secure full economic recovery for the nation. Unemployment remained a problem, and production never neared capacity, until the Second World War. It did however restore national self-confidence and caused a reassertion of faith in democracy.

The New Deal, and its creator, permanently altered the nature of the presidency, and of American government. FDR not only gave energy to government but in an age of dawning public awareness of, and involvement in, public affairs he gave to its activities vividness and drama. The word "charisma" had to wait for a television age, but he had it in abundance. It was as if there were a man in the White House who had an extra dimension, and a special zest for life. Rexford Tugwell said that he was "not a made president, but a born one. . . . No monarch . . . unless it may have been Elizabeth or her magnificent Tudor father, or maybe Alexander or Augustus Caesar, can have quite given that sense of serene presiding, of gathering up into himself, or really representing, a whole people. He had a right to his leeways, he had a right to use everyone in his own way, he had every right to manage and manipulate the palpables and impalpables. . . . He had touch with something deeper than reason."

As the New Deal came to a close, President Roosevelt addressed the nation in the elections of 1938. FDR could look back on an epoch-making period of legislative improvisation and inspired leadership. Hardly any aspect of the economy had been overlooked—from agriculture to banking to industry—and neither was the workingman. American life had been revamped, and the federal government began to assume the responsibilities of a modern welfare state. The worst of the slump was over: America had survived the Great Depression.

Franklin D Roosevelt Library

Bibliography

GENERAL

Blum, John M., *From the Morgenthau Diaries: Years of Crisis, 1928-1938* (Boston, 1959)

Braeman, John, *et al.*, eds., *The New Deal* 2 vols, (Columbus, Oh., 1975)

Brogan, Denis W., *The Era of Franklin D. Roosevelt* (New Haven, 1950)

Burns, James MacGregor, *Roosevelt: The Lion and the Fox* (New York, 1956)

Freidel, Frank, *Franklin D. Roosevelt* (4 vols., to date, Boston, 1952-1974)

Goldman, Eric F., *Rendezvous with Destiny: A History of Modern American Reform* (New York, 1952)

Leuchtenburg, William E., *Franklin D. Roosevelt and the New Deal, 1932-1940* (New York, 1963)

McCoy, Donald R., *Coming of Age: The United States during the 1920's and 1930's* (Harmondsworth, Middlesex, & Baltimore, 1973)

McElvaine, Robert S., *The Great Depression: America, 1929-1941* (New York, 1984)

Mitchell, Broadus, *Depression Decade* (New York, 1947)

Moley, Raymond, *After Seven Years* (New York, 1939)

Perkins, Dexter, *The New Age of Franklin Roosevelt, 1932-45* (Chicago, 1957)

Rauch, Basil, *The History of the New Deal* (New York, 1944)

Robinson, Edgar E., *The Roosevelt Leadership, 1933-1945* (Philadelphia, 1955)

Schlesinger, Arthur M., Jr., *The Age of Roosevelt* (3 vols., Boston, 1957-60)

Chapter 1: A NATION IN DESPAIR

Daniels, Roger V., *The Bonus March* (Westport, Conn., 1971)

Lyons, Eugene, *Herbert Hoover, A Biography* (Garden City, N.Y., 1964)

Romasco, Albert U., *The Poverty of Abundance: Hoover, the Nation, the Depression* (New York, 1965)

Schwarz, Jordan A., *The Interregnum of Despair: Hoover, Congress and the Depression* (Urbana, Ill., 1970)

Temin, Peter, *Did Monetary Forces Cause the Great Depression?* (New York, 1976)

Warren, Harris G., *Herbert Hoover and the Great Depression* (New York, 1959)

Chapter 2: NOTHING TO FEAR

A Mandate for Recovery

Brennan, John A., *Silver and the First New Deal* (Reno, Nev., 1969)

Charles, Searle F., *Minister of Relief: Harry Hopkins and the Depression* (Syracuse, N.Y., 1963)

Clapp, Gordon R., *The TVA: An Approach to the Development of a Region* (Chicago, 1955)

Conkin, Paul K., *Tomorrow a New World: The New Deal Community Program* (Ithaca, N.Y., 1959)

de Bedts, Ralph F., *The New Deal's SEC: The Formative Years* (New York, 1964)

Hawley, Ellis W., *The New Deal and the Problem of Monopoly* (Princeton, 1966)

Jackson, Charles O., *Food and Drug Legislation in the New Deal* (Princeton, 1970)

Klein, Lawrence R., *The Keynesian Revolution* (New York, 1947)

McCraw, Thomas K., *TVA and the Power Fight, 1933-1939* (Philadelphia, 1971)

Parrish, Michael, *Securities Regulation and the New Deal* (New Haven, 1970)

Perkins, Van L., *Crisis in Agriculture: Agricultural Adjustment and the New Deal, 1933* (Berkeley, Cal., 1969)

Romasco, Albert U., *The Politics of Recovery: Roosevelt's New Deal* (New York, 1983)

Salmond, John A., *The Civilian Conservation Corps, 1933-1942* (Durham, N.C., 1967)

Stein, Herbert, *The Fiscal Revolution in America* (Chicago, 1969)

Tugwell, Rexford G., *The Brains Trust* (New York, 1968)

Challenges to the New Deal

Alsop, Joseph, & Catledge, Turner, *The 168 Days* (Garden City, N.Y., 1938)

Bennett, David H., *Demagogues in the Depression: American Radicals and the Union Party, 1932-1936* (New Brunswick, N.Y., 1969)

Blackorby, Edward C., *Prairie Rebel: The Public Life of William Lemke* (Lincoln, Neb., 1963)

Boskin, Joseph, comp., *Opposition Politics: The Anti-New Deal Tradition* (Beverly Hills, Cal., 1968)

Brinkley, Alan, *Voices of Protest: Huey Long, Father Coughlin, and the Great Depression* (New York, 1982)

Eriksson, E. McK., *The Supreme Court and the New Deal* (Rosemead, Cal., 1941)

Fleischman, Harry, *Norman Thomas, A Biography* (New York, 1964)

Flynn, George Q., *American Catholics and the Roosevelt Presidency, 1932-1936* (Lexington, Ky., 1968)

Hendel, Samuel, *Charles Evans Hughes and the Supreme Court* (New York, 1951)

Holtzman, Abraham, *The Townsend Movement: A Political Study* (New York, 1963)

Huthmacher, J. Joseph, *Senator Robert F. Wagner and the Rise of Urban Liberalism* (New York, 1968)

Lubove, Roy, *The Struggle for Social Security, 1900-1935* (Cambridge, Mass., 1968)

McCoy, Donald R., *Angry Voices: Left-of-center Politics in the New Deal Era* (Lawrence, Kan., 1958)

McCoy, Donald R., *Landon of Kansas* (Lincoln, Neb., 1966)

Polenberg, Richard, "The National Committee to Uphold Constitutional Government, 1937-1941," *Journal of American History,* 52 (1965)

Tull, Charles J., *Father Coughlin and the New Deal* (Syracuse, N.Y., 1965)

Warren, Frank A., III, *Liberals and Communism: The 'Red Decade' Revisited* (Bloomington, Ind., 1966)

Williams, T. Harry, *Huey Long* (New York, 1969)

Witte, Edwin E., *The Development of the Social Security Act* (Madison, 1962)

Wolfskill, George, *The Revolt of the Conservatives: The American Liberty League, 1934-1940* (Boston, 1962)

Wolfskill, George, & Hudson, John A., *All But the People: Franklin D. Roosevelt and His Critics, 1933-1939* (New York, 1969)

Chapter 3: SOCIETY DURING THE DEPRESSION

Caro, Robert A., *The Power Broker: Robert Moses and the Fall of New York* (New York, 1974)

Davie, Maurice R., *Refugees in America* (New York, 1947)

Fishel, Leslie H., Jr., "The Negro in the New Deal Era," *Wisconsin Magazine of History,* 48 (1964)

Lange, Dorothea, & Taylor, Paul S., *American Exodus: Human Erosion in the Thirties* (rev. edn., New Haven, 1969)

McWilliams, Carey, *Factories in the Field: The Story of Migratory Farm Labor in California* (Boston, 1939)

Mann, Arthur, *La Guardia Comes to Power, 1933* (Chicago, 1965)

Ribuffo, Leo, *The Old Christian Right: The Protestant Far Right from the Great Depression to the Cold War* (Philadelphia, 1983)

Trout, Charles H., *Boston, The Great Depression, and the New Deal* (New York, 1977)

Waples, Douglas, *Peoples and Print: Social Aspects of Reading in the Depression* (Chicago, 1937)

Ware, Susan, *Beyond Suffrage: Women in the New Deal* (Cambridge, Mass., 1981)

Wecter, Dixon, *Age of the Great Depression* (New York, 1948)

Weiss, Nancy J., *Farewell to the Party of Lincoln: Black Politics in the Age of F.D.R.* (Princeton, N.J., 1983)

Wolters, Raymond, *Negroes and the Great Depression: The Problem of Economic Recovery* (Westport, Conn., 1973)

Young, Donald, *Research Memorandum on Minority Peoples in the Depression* (New York, 1937)

Chapter 4: ART, ANGER, AND ESCAPE

Aaron, Daniel, *Writers on the Left: Episodes in American Literary Communism* (New York, 1961)

Barnouw, Erik, *History of Broadcasting in the United States* (3 vols., New York, 1966-70)

Blesh, Rudi, *Modern Art USA: Men, Rebellion, Conquest, 1900-1956* (New York, 1956)

Bogan, Louise, *Achievement in American Poetry, 1900-1950* (Chicago, 1951)

Burlingame, Roger, *Don't Let Them Scare You: The Life and Times of Elmer Davis* (Philadelphia, 1961)

Ewen, David, *Journey to Greatness: The Life and Music of George Gershwin* (New York, 1956)

Flexner, Eleanor, *American Playwrights, 1918-1938* (New York, 1938)

Geismar, Maxwell D., *Writers in Crisis: The American Novel Between Two Wars* (Boston, 1942)

Goodman, Benny, & Kolodin, Irving, *The Kingdom of Swing* (New York, 1939)

Himelstein, Morgan Y., *Drama Was A Weapon: Left Wing Theater in New York, 1929-1941* (New Brunswick, N.J., 1963)

Ludington, Townsend, *John Dos Passos: A Twentieth-Century Odyssey* (New York, 1980)

McKinzie, Richard D., *The New Deal for Artists* (Princeton, 1973)

Marling, Karal A., *Wall-to-Wall America: A Cultural History of Post-Office Murals in the Great Depression* (Minneapolis, Minn., 1982)

Mathews, Jane D., *The Federal Theater, 1935-1939* (Princeton, 1967)

Mock, Elizabeth, ed., *Built in USA, 1932-1944* (New York, 1944)

Penkower, Monty N., *The Federal Writers' Project: A Study in Government Patronage of the Arts* (Urbana, Ill., 1977)

Rideout, Walter B., *The Radical Novel in the United States, 1900-1954* (Cambridge, Mass., 1956)

Rose, Barbara, *American Art Since 1900: A Critical History* (London, 1967)

Smith, Julia F., *Aaron Copland, His Work and Contribution to American Music* (New York, 1955)

Thorp, Margaret, *America at the Movies* (New Haven, 1939)

Thorp, Willard, *American Writing in the Twentieth Century* (Cambridge, Mass., 1960)

Wagenknecht, Edward, *Movies in the Age of Innocence* (Norman, Okla., 1962)

Chapter 5: MAKING RECOVERY WORK

The Right to Organize

Alinsky, Saul D., *John L. Lewis, An Unauthorized Biography* (New York, 1949)

Bernstein, Irving, *The New Deal Collective Bargaining Policy* (Berkeley, Cal., 1950)

Bernstein, Irving, *Turbulent Years: A History of the American Worker, 1933-1941* (Boston, 1970)

Cortner, Richard C., *The Wagner Act Cases* (Knoxville, Tenn., 1964)

Dubofsky, Melvyn & Van Tine, Warren, *John L. Lewis* (New York, 1977)

Fine, Sidney, *The Automobile Under The Blue Eagle* (Ann Arbor, 1963)

Fine, Sidney, *Sit-Down: The General Motors Strike of 1936-1937* (Ann Arbor, 1969)

Galenson, Walter, *The CIO Challenge to the AFL* (Cambridge, Mass., 1960)

Josephson, Matthew, *Sidney Hillman, Statesman of American Labor* (Garden City, N.Y., 1952)

McFarland, Charles K., *Roosevelt, Lewis and the New Deal, 1933-1940* (Fort Worth, Texas, 1970)

Millis, Harry A., & Brown, E. C., *From the Wagner Act to Taft-Hartley* (Chicago, 1950)

Young, Edwin, & Derber, Milton, eds., *Labor and the New Deal* (Madison, 1957)

The Farmer's Plight

Albertson, Dean, *Roosevelt's Farmer: Claude R. Wickard in the New Deal* (New York, 1961)

Baldwin, Sidney, *Poverty and Politics: The Rise and Decline of the Farm Security Administration* (Chapel Hill, N.C., 1968)

Campbell, Christiana M., *The Farm Bureau and the New Deal* (Urbana, Ill., 1962)

Cantor, Louis, *Prologue to the Protest Movement: The Missouri Sharecropper Roadside Demonstration of 1939* (Durham, N.C., 1969)

Conrad, David E., *Forgotten Farmers: The Story of Sharecroppers in the New Deal* (Urbana, Ill., 1965)

Fite, Gilbert C., *George N. Peek and the Fight for Farm Parity* (Norman, Okla., 1954)

Kirkendall, Richard S., *Social Scientists and Farm Politics in the Age of Roosevelt* (Columbia, Mo., 1966)

Rowley, William D., *M. L. Wilson and the Campaign for the Domestic Allotment* (Lincoln, Neb., 1970)

Schapsmeier, Edward L. & Frederick H., *Henry A. Wallace of Iowa, 1910-1965* (2 vols., Ames, Iowa, 1968-70)

Shover, John L., *Cornbelt Rebellion: The Farmers' Holiday Association* (Urbana, Ill., 1965)

Worster, Donald, *Dust Bowl: The Southern Plains in the 1930s* (New York, 1979)

Chapter 6: PRESERVING THE AMERICAN SYSTEM

Ekirch, Arthur A., Jr., *Ideologies and Utopias: The Impact of the New Deal on American Thought* (Chicago, 1969)

Graham, Otis L., Jr., *Toward a Planned Society: From Roosevelt to Nixon* (New York, 1976)

Hirshfield, Daniel S., *Lost Reform: The Campaign for Compulsory Medical Insurance in the United States from 1932-1943* (Cambridge, Mass., 1970)

Patterson, James T., *Congressional Conservatism and the New Deal* (Lexington, Ky., 1967)

Patterson, James T., *The New Deal and the States: Federalism in Transition* (Princeton, 1969)

Polenberg, Richard D., *Reorganizing Roosevelt's Government: The Controversy over Executive Reorganization, 1936-1939* (Cambridge, Mass., 1966)

Roose, Kenneth D., *The Economics of Recession and Revival: An Interpretation of 1937-1938* (New Haven, 1954)